THE FULLNESS OF LIFE

THE FULLNESS OF LIFE

RELECTIONS ON THE LORD'S PRAYER
FOR TODAY'S WORLD

MICHAEL SMITH

Initiatives of Change

Published 2012 by
Initiatives of Change UK
24 Greencoat Place
London SW1P 1RD

Text and cover design by Blair Cummock
Typeset in Sabon 10.5 pt
Cover photo: Richard Seah

ISBN 978-1-85239-045-7

Printed and bound in the UK by Biddles,
part of the MPG Books Group
Bodmin and King's Lynn

Every day it's a getting closer
Going faster than a roller coaster,
Love like yours will surely come my way.
                              Buddy Holly

Motor of love, motor of love,
Heavenly father look down from above.
I can't get over your powerful
Motor of love.
                              Paul McCartney

Forewords

Many books have been published about the Lord's Prayer, but few which are as fresh as this collection of Michael Smith's meditations on the text of Christ's exemplary prayer, that prayer of the Kingdom which he gave to his disciples in response to their request that Jesus should teach them to pray. Throughout, Michael shares something of his own spiritual journey and experiences through this interaction between the way we pray and the way we live, challenged as we are by the 'agenda' of the Lord's Prayer.

In this deceptively understated and small book, Michael tells how the application of this 'universal' prayer to his own particular situation challenged and transformed the direction of his life, especially in his late, turbulent teenage years. The passages about temptation, forgiveness and the ongoing power of evil are especially telling and relate with real insight to so many of the issues facing our contemporary world.

The questions for discussion, either in a group or for personal reflection at the end of each section, are especially helpful and incisive. It is the kind of book which not only speaks to Christians or to churchgoers, but which would also speak to 'seekers' or to the many people today who are searching for a deeper meaning to life and yet who have not connected with the worshipping and praying community of the Church.

The Rt Revd Michael Marshall
President, The Awareness Foundation

When I was prisons minister I came into frequent contact with those who had not been on their guard against being led into evil, who had no notion that they were empowered to say 'no' to temptation, who neither forgave nor sought forgiveness. As this book observes, their chaplains work hard but still they re-appear for another sentence. There was a time when every child was taught the Lord's Prayer and what it meant. It is, in short, the best preparation for life itself. I wish this book was in every school library.

Ann Widdecombe
Minister for Prisons, 1995-1997

Mike is a solid nonconformist Christian of the United Reformed Church, whom I have known for 20 years. He lives out his Christian faith in the difficult world of politics and finance. These *Reflections* reflect Mike's deep commitment to the understanding of the universality of God's message of reassurance and love and deserve a wide readership and audience. He is a layman, as am I, but the *Reflections* offer wisdom in depth on the Prayer we all turn to in our times of both trouble and thanksgiving.

Tony Colman
Labour MP for Putney, 1997-2005
Director africapractice; Councillor, World Future Council;
Accredited Local Preacher, UK Methodist Church

The Lord's Prayer is the most radical and subversive text ever written. In this well crafted book Mike Smith reconnects a modern audience with its deep truths and challenges. Read it, understand it, and then pray the Prayer if you're brave enough to do so.

James Featherby
Chair of the Church of England Ethical Investment
Advisory Group; author, of 'Of Markets and Men' and
'The White Swan Formula'.

Our Father,
Who art in heaven,
Hallowed be Thy name.
Thy Kingdom come.
Thy will be done,
On Earth, as it is in heaven.
Give us this day our daily bread
And forgive us our trespasses
As we forgive those who trespass against us.
Lead us not into temptation
But deliver us from evil,
For thine is the Kingdom, the power and the glory,
For ever and ever. Amen.

(Taken from Matthew 6, vv 9-13, and Luke 11, vv 2-4)

The origins of these reflections lie in a series of retreats at the convent of the Sisters of St Andrew in Edenbridge, Kent, which my wife and I attended in the early 2000s. They were organized by our friend and colleague, Mary Lean. As I walked in the gardens I found myself thinking at length about the collective nature of human existence, as expressed in the phrase 'Our Father', including its notion of solidarity and family virtue. I was also conscious that, while many of my generation, and countless generations earlier, had been brought up to recite the Lord's Prayer from an early age, learning it in home, school or church, few of us nowadays take the time or effort to ponder on the implications of what we say and too easily take for granted. I felt a growing urge to explore further the significance of the prayer that has been handed down from generation to generation. Several sources have been particularly helpful in my thinking, including *The Lord and His Prayer* by Tom Wright (1996); *Insights: the Lord's Prayer* by William Barclay (1975, republished 2008), *Jesus of Nazareth* by Pope Benedict XV1 (2007); *The Lord's Prayer for Modern Man* by Roger Hicks (1967); *The Lord's Prayer* by E F Scott (1951) and *The Transforming Power of Prayer* by Michael Marshall (2011). I am grateful for the insights and thinking of these scholars and theologians, of which I am neither.

Abbreviations in text:
ASV: Authorized Standard Version
ESV: English Standard Version
KJB: King James Bible
NEB: New English Bible
NIV: New International Version

Introduction

THERE IS A MOVING SCENE in the film *Master and Commander* when a ship's crew, led by the captain (played by Russell Crowe), commits to the deep the bodies of their fellow crew members following a sea battle. They have been killed in fierce hand-to-hand combat with French sailors during the Napoleonic Wars. The entire crew recites together the Lord's Prayer. With its notion of human solidarity, and acknowledgement of the divine presence, it is a stirring moment in the whole story.

The Lord's Prayer is, of course, not just said at times of human loss, at the death of loved ones. It does, however, help to build a bridge between us, still living, and the eternal world beyond death, if we hold any such belief in a life beyond life. Heaven is not that far away. Indeed, it is very close. One minute our loved ones are with us. The next they are taken from us. It is we who remain who have to cope with the grief of loss. The Lord's Prayer encompasses the notion of a loving God, a heavenly father, our father. In so doing it prepares us for heaven, for the world beyond death—the eternal world of time past, present and future.

Yet essentially the Lord's Prayer provides us with a road map for living in the here and now: a commitment to doing God's will, not our own, here on earth; our need for 'daily bread'; the resistance of temptation; the avoidance of evil; the acknowledgement of where power really lies. And in following this road map, we are not alone. We are all on the road together, in comradeship, in solidarity, in community: '*Our* Father....'; 'Give *us* this day *our* daily bread'; 'Lead *us*

not into temptation but deliver *us* from evil.... Our fulfillment lies not just in ourselves as loners but in being part of
a wider community, as were the followers of Jesus to whom
he first gave his prayer.

So what is the significance of the Lord's Prayer for
today's world? It is one of the most well known prayers,
and one of the most repeated texts, in human history. The
vast majority of the world's two billion Christians probably
know it by heart, brought up on it since childhood and, for
those who are regular church attenders, declaring it Sunday
by Sunday. Many of other faith traditions may also know it.
Yet far too many of today's generation, at least in Western
Europe, are brought up with hardly any knowledge of its
significance, as one of the central texts of the world's religious and cultural treasures. A March 2012 survey for BBC
TV's *Newsround* found that British children aged six to 12
are twice as likely to say that religion is important to them
compared with 40 years ago—but they are now only half as
likely to know the text of the Lord's Prayer. Part of this, of
course, may be explained by the increase in the number of
children of other faith traditions.

Many may know something of the great and dramatic
Biblical stories: Noah's ark and the great flood; the betrayal
of Joseph by his brothers to the Egyptians; the Israelites'
escape from Egypt across the Red Sea; Moses and the ten
commandments at Mount Ararat; the young David slaying
the giant Goliath; the wisdom and wealth of David's son,
King Solomon; Daniel being sent into the lion's den; Jonah
being swallowed up in the belly of the whale; the birth of
Jesus to Mary in Bethlehem and the visit of the wise men
from the East with their gifts of gold, frankincense and
myrrh; the great parables of Jesus, encasing home truths.
These are all part of the world's great cultural heritage. So
too is the Lord's Prayer. Yet even for those who have a
strong knowledge of it, the Lord's Prayer can be a mantra

that loses its meaning and impact—too easy to recite without thought.* Yet in today's secular and materialistic culture, the great prayer has the power to be radically subversive, reflecting Christ's own persona, in challenging and changing the prevailing social mores.

It was given by Jesus in response to a request from the disciples—his immediate followers. As William Barclay points out, it was meant initially and primarily for them rather than for the wider mass of people. 'The Lord's Prayer can only really be prayed when those who pray it know what they are saying....' (Barclay, *The Lord's Prayer*, 2008). Yet it is, suggests E F Scott (*The Lord's Prayer*, 1951), 'the primary Christian document, and the only one which comes directly from Jesus himself.' He wrote nothing himself 'and all that we know of his message is through the reports of others. But he was himself the author of this prayer, and took care to write it indelibly on the memories of his disciples'.

One can speculate whether or not Jesus anticipated the moment when the disciples would ask him how to pray. He may well have given it thought and waited till they asked the question: 'Lord, teach us how to pray.' Whatever the circumstances, the Lord's Prayer cannot be regarded as off-the-cuff. The use of words, including story-telling in his parables, mattered supremely to Jesus. He was the master of the sound-bite. In the few choice phrases of his prayer, he presents a whole philosophy of life. Indeed, the Lord's Prayer is so profound that it repays study and reflection. If we allow it to, it has the power to change our lives, alter our perceptions of reality, and create destinies. For our habits

---

* Even here we should be wary of denigrating the notion of mantra. Sister Ruth Burrows points out that 'To repeat a mantra (ie a short prayer) can be an excellent way of helping us to focus on receiving God's love.' (*Essence of Prayer*, Burns & Oats, 2006).

create our destinies. As the old saying goes, our thoughts lead to actions, our actions to habits, our habits to character, and our character to our destiny.

Most of the things we might want to pray about are taken care of within the Lord's Prayer, says Tom Wright (*Simply Christian*, 2006). 'Like Jesus' parables, it is small in scale but huge in coverage. Some people find it helpful to pray it slowly, pausing every few words to hold before God the particular things on our hearts which come into that category. Some people prefer to use it either at the beginning or the end of a more extended time of prayer, either to set the context for everything else or to sum it up. Some people find that saying it slowly, over and over again, helps them to go down deeply into the love and presence of God, into the place where the spheres overlap, into the power of the gospel to bring bread and forgiveness and rescue. However you want to use it, use it. Start here and see where it takes you.'

1. Our Father

IT IS SO EASY to take the opening words for granted. But what might first surprise us about the Lord's Prayer are indeed its opening two words—*Our Father*. Surprising because addressing God in this way puts us into a uniquely personal, intimate relationship with God. Why 'Father'? Why not 'Divine Creator'? Or 'Supreme Being'? Or 'the intelligence behind the Universe'? Or any of the other ways that we might want to describe God?

Years ago when I was a teenager, I asked the astronomer and broadcaster Patrick Moore, a neighbour in my home village, if I could see the sky at night through his telescopes. He pointed to one star and asked how far away I thought it was. I hadn't a clue. Well, he said, the light you are seeing left that star at the time of William the Conqueror a thousand years ago and is just reaching us now. I asked him if he believed there was a God who had created the stars and the galaxies. He affirmed his belief that there must be an intelligence behind the whole of creation, but did not at that time admit to a belief in a personal God. So did he, as he studied the galaxies, ever feel himself to be lord and master of it all? 'Good heavens, no,' he replied. 'Not at all. Very humbling, very humbling.'

So why 'Father'? Is this not just a human construct—a way of bringing God down to our tiny scale as individuals on a small planet in one spot of the vast universe?

Far from it. From the very outset, Jesus establishes the pattern of an anthropomorphic relationship between God the creator, God the Father and us, therefore, his children.

It is essentially relational, as reflected in the family relationship—the basic, core human model for the ordering of society which, according to recent research and discovery, dates back to the Stone Age. Then the family unit may have been a question of survival. Today, it is the cornerstone of companionship, commitment and continuity from one generation to the next.

In emphasizing this personal relationship with God, Jesus also, by inference, establishes the family unit as reflecting the divine will. Here, then, is not a remote, unknown or unknowable entity at all but just the opposite. Here is a God who cares for each of us intimately, personally and individually.

Assuming the model of fatherhood that *should be*, rather than often *is*, here is a God who loves us; who hugs us, looks after us, smiles at us and ruffles our hair, who picks us up when we fall and puts us on our feet again, who provides for all our needs and, like all good fathers, educates us—and corrects us when we need correcting. And he does all this differently for each one of us. Each of our personalities and needs are different from everyone else's. A God, then, who is accessible on our human scale, to whom we run like children and who comes not ambling but running, almost sprinting, towards us as we, his prodigal children, turn or return to him. For each of us he has our personal interests uniquely at heart.

Jesus, who was particularly aware of the uniqueness of his personal relationship with God—through the divine nature of his birth—called God 'Abba' which in Aramaic meant Daddy, they were on such close personal terms. 'Abba,' says C H Dodd, 'was the intimate mode of address from child to father in the Jewish family.' (*The Founder of Christianity*, 1971)

Can we ascribe emotion to God? Why not? He is a loving Father, and we can also assume that he hurts with our hurts—whether at times of illness, pain, suffering, through our own fault or the sins and wickedness of others inflicted on us—and rejoices with our triumphs. As Ray Simpson comments in his book *The Cowshed Revolution* (2011), 'God could not communicate himself to a finite being if he did not already have the capacity within himself to give and receive love.' Indeed, it is often said that 'God is love'. A good father has compassion. He empathizes with our ups and downs in life. He brings comfort as we turn to him.

As he does this for each one of us he also reminds us of the relationship all of us on planet Earth have with each other. If he is *our* father then we are all brothers and sisters. Muslims tend to call each other as such much more than Christians. But Jesus reminds us in the first two words of the Lord's Prayer that we are in relationship with each other. If Jesus called God *Abba* or Daddy, then he seemed to be inviting us to regard him, Jesus, as our brother. As Michael Marshall writes: 'When Jesus was asked to give a lesson on prayer, he urged us to begin, not with "My Father", but rather with "*Our* Father". This has wild implications, and not only for prayer and praying. In effect, Jesus is saying, "When you pray, always pray together with me your brother, and let us pray together to *our Father*." Such teaching and practice is even more revolutionary when we consider that Jesus was teaching this to Jews, for whom the very name of God was unmentionable. Now we are instructed by Jesus, together with him as our brother, and through his Holy Spirit, to address the unspeakable and unnamed God "Abba"—"Daddy". To Jews, as well as to Muslims and many others, such a form of address would be little short of blasphemy.'

Michael Marshall continues that the developing relationship with God 'our Father' is mirrored in the maturing relationship between children and their parents. 'Often, as children grow up, they become the friends of their parents as mature men and women. It would seem from the teaching of Jesus that God also desires that amazing development towards what we might want to call a mature relationship with God our Father.' (*The Transforming Power of Prayer: from Illusion to Reality*, 2011)

There is more to consider. The disciple Philip says to Jesus, 'Lord, show us the Father and that will be enough for us.' (John 14, v 8, NIV). In his reply Jesus emphatically relates himself to equality with the Father. 'Don't you know me, Philip, even after I have been among you such a long time? Anyone who has seen me has seen the Father. How can you say, "Show us the Father"? Don't you believe that I am in the Father and that the Father is in me? The words I say to you are not just my own. Rather it is the Father, living in me, who is doing his work.' (John 14, vv 9-10, NIV). Jesus becomes the model for our understanding of the Father. Yet at the same time, and paradoxically, Jesus in his humility does not put himself on the same level of importance as the Father. As he prepares for his anticipated crucifixion Jesus tells his disciples: 'If you loved me you would be glad that I am going to the Father, for the Father is greater than I.' (John 14, v 28, NIV) (We needn't here go further into theological issues over the nature of the relationship between God the father and God the son.)

Moreover, if God is our father, and the father to all generations, then he is also the source of life and continuity. Without fatherhood there is no life. He, then, is the source of life. We were, in one sense, simply the figments of his imagination before we existed in flesh and bone, so intriguingly and beautifully suggested in Jostein Gaarder's novel about the great philosophers, *Sophie's World* (1995). We are all wanted children, whatever the circumstances of our human parentage. God has willed us into existence. He is a pro-creational God, and a prolific one at that. As Pope Benedict XVI points out, 'The sign of God is overflowing generosity. We see it in the multiplication of the loaves [in the story of Jesus feeding the crowd of 5,000]; we see it again and again—most of all though, at the centre of salvation history [the story of Jesus' life on Earth], in the fact that he lavishly spends himself for the lowly creature, man. This abundant giving is his 'glory'. This superabundance of Cana [in Jesus' first miracle when he turns water into wine at the wedding feast in Cana] is therefore a sign that God's feast with humanity, his self-giving for men, has begun.' (*Jesus of Nazareth*, 2007)

Of course many grow up with role models of fatherhood that are distorted—angry, abusive, violent, exploitative, extortionate, disturbed. Such corrupted role models have to be overcome, to be healed and redeemed, so that we can begin to understand and experience the model of fatherhood as it should be—loving, forgiving, encouraging and attentive. Moreover, we may all have to leave, at some time or another, the controlling aspect of our human, biological fathers and mothers in order to find our true relationship with the divine father. The Hollywood film *Dead Poets Society* (1989) showed a son who cannot break free from the domination of his human father, with tragic consequences. As Michael Marshall writes, 'wherever those family ties inhibit growth and hold us back, they need to be cut in order to release us to play our part in the larger community. For the family is intended to be the basic building block, but always in order to enable a larger building—community and society. So in the teaching of Jesus... he is, in effect, saying that we 'honour father and mother' best when we grow beyond them as sons and daughters, and as we become their mature friends in the wider family of the community.' (*The Transforming Power of Prayer: from Illusion to Reality*, 2011)

Kevin Scott, West End musical singer, photographer, film maker and author, tells the story of his own experience:

When I was 12 years old, my father returned from work angry about something. He grumbled at me and removed his leather belt. I knew he was going to thrash me. I would never talk back to my father, but shouted, 'You're a bully!' His face turned blue with rage. He raised his hands to grab me. I thought he might kill me and fled from the house.

On a hillside overlooking San Francisco Bay I lay down in tall grass to catch my breath and ponder what to do. I feared returning home. I wondered why my father directed his anger at me. I thought fathers were supposed to love and protect their children. Then something warm touched my chest, went into my body and caressed my heart. A calm, masculine voice said, 'You belong to me.' I jumped up and looked around. Nobody was there. I lay down again. Fear disappeared. I went home, entering through the back door. Father sat at the dining room table, a bottle of whisky in one hand and a glass in the other. He glowered at me but didn't speak. I slipped into the bedroom shared with my brothers.

I spent years trying to discover who or what had replaced fear with a certainty of being loved and protected. There was no logical explanation, yet the experience left an indelible impression. Psychologists will say that I had an hallucination resulting from the trauma of being severely frightened by my father's rage and fear that he would have killed me had I not fled. That is undeniably a rational scientific explanation. However the voice I heard—once only in my life—said nothing other than those four words. It made no demands. No 'In return for this, you owe me....' I never felt controlled or under any obligation. Nor have I claimed it was the voice of God or the Holy Spirit, however much I was inclined to think so. What I later heard about Jesus came closer than anything to explain my experience. Yet, to be honest, I have no evidence to support that hypothesis. I have not found absolute truth in any doctrine or ideology but am beginning to learn from deep within.*

So where does this leave motherhood? In the natural, created world, there can be no fatherhood without motherhood. Why did Jesus address God as Father and not Mother? Does he simply leave it up to our imagination to realize the dual nature of God as father and mother? In the culture in which Jesus lived, fathers were essentially the breadwinners, the providers. God is the great provider. But mothers are the great givers of life. And in the Roman Catholic tradition Jesus' mother, Mary—the Blessed Virgin Mary—is uniquely honoured amongst women. We perhaps have to assume that in the nature of God himself, the great creator and provider, the great giver of life, there is a duality of gender, if gender means anything at all in a divine context.

Here, then, is God as fatherhood to perfection. Not God as a remote, distant figure but God as a knowable, personal father who has our best interests at heart; a God whom we can trust and by whom we are greatly loved.

But in regarding God as such, we are also left reflecting on the nature and quality of our relationship with our biological fathers, even as and when they are loving. This, of course, varies enormously from person to person. And whether we are fathers or children, or both, there comes a point where we begin to recognize that earthly fathers are fallible—that none are perfect, human nature being what it is. (We shall come back to family relationships when we address the section of the Lord's Prayer on forgiveness.) But we can have the confidence that in the fatherhood of God lies perfection.

---

* www.iofc.org/you_belong_to_me 16.05.2011

QUESTIONS:
How do I see fatherhood? Motherhood?
What is/was my relationship with my father like?
How do I see my relationship with God?
What is the significance of the word 'Our' in this opening
*   phrase?*

2. Who art in heaven

I LIKE the use of the old-fashioned English. Modern translations tend to simplify: 'Our father in heaven'. What? As opposed to our fathers on Earth? There is a stronger emphasis in 'Our Father who art in heaven.' This is a categorical statement. God is definitely in heaven. This is where he resides. No doubt about it.

So what is our notion of heaven? How do we imagine it? Is it somewhere else from where we are now? We often regard it as the place we go to when we die, if we have any belief in an afterlife, and if we have been good enough to be welcomed there. When my mother died at the age of 93, I phoned our daughter and said, 'Granny's gone to heaven.' This was much more than just a way of coping with her death and our loss. It was an expression of faith, a belief in life after death. Heaven is the better place we hope to attain in the next life: the place of rest, of divine bliss, of perfection, of complete contentment, where our fears, worries and anxieties are over; somewhere else than where we live on this earth. It is the place where our Father resides, and where, if we have the faith, we hope we shall meet up again with our loved ones.

But wait on. Haven't we said that our Father is indeed incredibly close to us, even as we live on this earth? And if he lives in heaven then heaven too is exceedingly close to us, or has the potential to be, even here on earth. As James Jones, the Bishop of Liverpool, puts it, 'Jesus was not only earthed but also saw his mission as none other than the earthing of heaven.' (*Jesus and the Earth,* 2003)

So Jesus has an entirely different take on heaven than the notion of 'somewhere else'. He tells the Pharisees (a Jewish school of thought) that 'the kingdom of heaven is within you.' (Luke 17, v 21). This is often translated as 'the kingdom of God is within you' (NIV) or indeed 'amongst you'. The point is, it's not 'out there'. It is right here, in the here and now. One can picture Jesus pointing to the heart or indeed the temple of his skull, or with an inclusive sweep of his arms. And as Jesus tells this to the Pharisees, he is making the point that he himself is amongst them. The kingdom of heaven is much more a state of mind, a presence, than only a place we go to when we die. Or to put it another way, the kingdom of heaven—or indeed hell—is as close to us as the synapses in our brains.

The late Jim Sullivan, a priest for some 70 years, said at his diamond jubilee: 'I spent the first 30 years of my priesthood trying to bring people into the kingdom. I've spent the last 30 years trying to bring the kingdom into people.' (Quoted by Monsignor Roderick Strange, Credo column, *The Times*, 16 July 2011.)

In one sense the whole of our lives are a journey to discover this kingdom of heaven that is within. We begin to discover it as we fulfill the conditions for discovering it: loving instead of hating, sharing instead of accumulating, serving instead of exploiting, healing instead of wounding, and creating peace instead of warfare. Old habits that distance ourselves from this heaven have to be unlearnt or overruled by habits that bring us closer to this heaven.

QUESTIONS:
What is my concept of heaven?
How do I picture it?
Where is heaven?

3. Hallowed be thy name

HALLOWED is the old word for praised or honoured. 'From the rising of the sun to the place where it sets, the name of the Lord is to be praised,' says Psalm 113 (NIV). The whole psalm is a call to praise the name of the Lord. Indeed a number of the Psalms of King David encourage us to 'praise God', to hallow his name, and this section of the Lord's Prayer picks up on these earlier psalms.

Psalm 117 (NIV):
Praise the Lord, all you nations,
extol him, all you peoples,
for great is his love towards us,
and the faithfulness of the Lord endures for ever.
Praise the Lord.

Psalm 111 (NIV):
Praise the Lord.
I will extol the Lord with all my heart in the council of
the upright and in the assembly.

Psalm 118 (NIV):
Give thanks to the Lord, for he is good;
His love endures for ever.

Equally, the General Thanksgiving in the Book of Common Prayer (1662) states: 'We bless thee for our creation, preservation, and all the blessings of this life... for the means of grace and the hope of glory.'

We can ask ourselves, therefore, who do we most hold in honour? Who do we adulate or praise? We talk about 'adoring' our loved ones, as if we worship the very ground they stand on. Yet we also know that we, and they, can disappoint. There inevitably comes a time when we simply fail to live up to others' expectations of us, whether in family or workplace relationships.

We live in an age of celebrity, from sports, movie and pop stars to politicians, presidents and prime ministers. We hold them in special honour, and then reserve the right to criticize them mercilessly when they fail to live up to our impossible expectations of them. Or we simply want to claim honours for ourselves.

It is, of course, good to praise and give honour to great public figures—to celebrate their achievements; to erect statues in their memory. As Michael Marshall points out, 'Looking up to others can, if properly handled by all concerned, help us to "grow up",' so long as we don't get stuck and 'turn icons into idols or signposts into finishing posts—mistaking those "resting places" of which Jesus speaks for our ultimate destination.' (*The Transforming Power of Prayer*, 2011)

Indeed, it is all too easy to idolize people—and in a media-savvy world to tear them down to our size when they disappoint. As the old saying goes, we treat some people as gods and others as dogs. And when our idols turn out to have feet of clay we become disillusioned. We begin to realize that we have treated them, in John Lennon's youthful brag, as 'more famous than Jesus'.

We can't believe it, for instance, when trusted bankers and financial investors put millions of dollars into artificial pyramid schemes, or promote reckless lending in unsustainable sub-prime mortgage markets, only for them to crash and our disillusionment to set in. We have 'hallowed' the wrong god. The Americans even print 'In God we trust' on their dollar notes. Far too many of us put our faith in the dollar, the pound or the euro, ignoring St Paul's warning that 'the love of money is a root of all kinds of evil' (1 Timothy 6, v 10, NIV).

When I was eight years old my parents sent me away to a boarding school. It meant that, for years, I lived in a state of fluctuating emotions—of elation as the end of term approached and dread as the end of the holidays and the return to school loomed. Fear, then relief, then fear again became an underlying rollercoaster of my childhood years. I bit my finger nails to the quick. You could say that I was a victim of my privileged background, though I never rationalized it as such at the time.

At the end of the half-term holidays, during my first term away from home at that tender age, I remember standing in our garden and sobbing. I simply didn't want to leave home again, however much my parents saw this as the best for me. My mother, in her deep sense of concern, said in great tenderness, 'Don't worry, God will look after you.' This simple remark had an electrifying effect on me. I felt a wave of relief run through my whole body, from head to toe. It was a palpable, physical experience. It was as if I could feel the blood coursing through my veins. For the first time in my life, I realized that there was someone in life who was more important than the headmaster (a kindly but daunting figure with a round face, dark and bushy eyebrows, and a pipe in his mouth). Yes, God would look after me. I look back on that experience and know that I can pinpoint it as the moment when faith in God became real to me. You could say it was a psychological experience that was right for that moment. But it never wholly left me. It certainly didn't mean that I was free from fear from then on, far from it. But somehow I knew, from that day on, that there was the fact of God, whose name is to be hallowed above all else—a God who was the most important entity in the universe. And indeed I grew to enjoy the school too.

A key word in this phrase *Hallowed be thy name* is 'thy'. It is a word of familiarity, lost in modern translations, similar to the use of *tu* or *ton* in French to mean you or your, when referring to a close relative or loved one, as opposed to *vous* or *votre* for more formal relationships. Once again, we are reminded that we are in a close and loving relationship with God. But, above all else, a God who is hallowed, who is praised, and whom we know does not disappoint but is utterly reliable.

So there is the simple, and profound, pleasure in 'hallowing' or praising God; giving thanks to him. Our thoughts can turn to the great creator in the presence of the great beauty of nature, from dramatic sunsets to spectacular views; in the beauty of flowers and the extraordinary range of animals; in the song and flight of birds; in the starlit sky at night; in great music; in the unsullied smiles in people's eyes; in the shared laughter of friends; and the delight and innocent joy of children at play. *Hallowed be thy name* sets us in the right frame of mind for the rest of the great prayer.

'The most liberating moment comes when we realize there is no one-size-fits-all prayer methodology,' writes the investment banker Ken Costa in his book *God at work* (2007). 'We all need to pray but the way that we do so should reflect the rich variety of God's ways of speaking to us. One way I find most powerful is the prayer of praise. Praise is our weapon of first resort. We can live under pressure if our perspective of God is right. Our understanding of the greatness of God leads us to despair of our own strength and to turn to God, the only one who can make sense of the complex world he has created. Praise is the war cry of the Christian asserting God's supremacy over the whole of life including the workplace.'

There are two other aspects to consider about this phrase *Hallowed be thy name*. First, it can be understood as a statement of liberation for the human spirit. In honouring God and his name, we need not be in thrall to the good opinion of others. It matters not one jot what other people think about us. This doesn't mean that we can be reckless or cavalier towards the wisdom of others, but that what matters most is that we honour God and his name first. As King Solomon says at the beginning of the book of Proverbs, 'How does a man become wise? The first step is to trust and reverence the Lord.' (Proverbs 1, v 7.) What matters is not what I think of myself or what others think of me, but what God thinks of me. His opinion is what counts. By honouring God and his name we live in freedom from any craving for the good opinion of others, which is merely a form of self-centredness, and we begin to live in wisdom. As the Psalmist declares: 'The Lord is my light and my salvation; whom should I fear? The Lord is the refuge of my life; of whom then should I go in dread?' (Psalm 27, v 1, NEB). As a teenager I used to be painfully shy and self-conscious; but as I grew up and gained the confidence of my convictions I found I was willing to engage without self-consciousness in conversation. The converse of this was that if anything was patently wrong in my convictions then I had to trust that my friends would say so and graciously accept their advice.

Secondly, honouring God and his name also gives God the credit for our successes. We so easily want to claim credit for ourselves, to boost our own egos. (And we shall come later to the issue of pride when we look at the temptations.) All that this does, though, is to make ourselves insufferable to others. Or, at its most extreme, turn us into tyrants. We too easily want to be 'the self-made man who worships his creator', which is the antithesis of humility. By hallowing God's name we unreservedly give God all the credit as well as all the honour and praise.

QUESTIONS:
Who or what do I hallow or hold in special honour?
Is this good or bad?
Why should we hallow God's name?
How do we hallow God's name?
*Do I live in fear of other people? If so, how can this be
      addressed?*

4. Thy Kingdom come

THERE WAS, in the years leading up to Jesus' birth, a huge sense of expectation amongst the Israelites that a saviour, or king, or liberator would be born to free them from Roman occupation.

The prophet Jeremiah had foretold it:

'The days are coming,' declares the Lord, 'when I will raise up to [King] David a righteous Branch, a King who will reign wisely and do what is just and right in the land. In his days Judah will be saved and Israel will live in safety. This is the name by which he will be called: The Lord Our Righteousness.' (Jeremiah 23, vv 5-6, NIV).

Jesus was born during the reign of King Herod, who had ruled Judea ruthlessly for 35 years on behalf of the Roman Emperor Caesar Augustus. Herod was definitely not the king foretold by Jeremiah; Herod ruled through fear and violence.

The prophet Isaiah was even more specific about the kind of king who would be born to liberate Israel:

The people walking in darkness have seen a great light; on those living in the land of the shadow of death a light has dawned. You have enlarged the nation and increased their joy; they rejoice before you as people rejoice at the harvest, as men rejoice when dividing the plunder. For as in the day of Midian's defeat, you have shattered the yoke that burdens them, the bar across their shoulders, the rod of their oppressor. Every warrior's boot used in battle and every garment rolled in blood will be destined for burning, will be fuel for the fire. For to us a child is born, to us a son

31

is given, and the government will be on his shoulders. And he will be called Wonderful, Counsellor, Mighty God, Everlasting Father, Prince of Peace. Of the increase of his government and peace there will be no end. He will reign on David's throne and over his kingdom, establishing and upholding it with justice and righteousness from that time on and forever. The zeal of the Lord Almighty will accomplish this. (Isaiah 9, vv 2-7, NIV)

It is in the context of these visionary, awe-inspiring prophesies that we begin to understand the notion of the Kingdom of God, and thus the prayer 'Thy Kingdom come', not just for Israel but for the whole of humanity.

It is also in this context that King Herod saw Jesus' birth as an immediate threat to his authority. When the Magi arrived in Jerusalem, their first question was: 'Where is the one who has been born king of the Jews? We saw his star in the East and have come to worship him.' St Matthew, who is the only gospel writer to tell the story of the Magi (Matthew 2, vv 1-12), reports that when King Herod heard their question he was disturbed 'and all Jerusalem with him'. And no wonder. The birth of a new king was an immediate challenge to the existing order. The Roman occupiers had a ruthless means of putting down any perceived threat. They crucified insurrectionists and their followers, in one instance lining them on their crosses along the route from Jericho to Jerusalem, a distance of 24 kilometres (15 miles).

With the birth of Jesus, the kingdom of God is upon us. In this historical context we can understand the notion of 'kingdom' rather than, say, empire or republic or presidency with which we are more familiar today. Jesus' birth became a challenge to the Judean kingdom.

King Herod was right to feel threatened. For the kingdom of God is a direct threat to all earthly power structures and tyrannies. As William Penn, the Quaker founder of the State

of Pennsylvania, said, 'People must choose to be governed
by God or they condemn themselves to be ruled by tyrants.'
If this sounds harsh it is because it implies that people get the
governments they deserve. It is, of course, a gross generaliza-
tion: it does not allow for the innocence of victims of other
people's venality, corruption and compromises with truth.
Can we really say that all the German people deserved
Hitler, or the Russians Stalin, or the Cambodians Pol Pot, or
the Iraqis Saddam Hussein? Hardly. Plenty of books have
been written about how such tyrants rose to power. And the
failures of human power structures played their part. But
while we can each choose to identify with the sins of our
forebears it is patently wrong for us to demand that others
accept a burden of guilt for their nation's history.

What we can say, with William Penn, is that the kingdom
of God is also the rule of freedom—in the human heart as
well as in the world's power structures. Even some of those
who have experienced the utter brutality of concentration
camps, from the Nazis to the Soviet Gulag, have witnessed
to an extraordinary inner freedom: when everything has
been taken away from you, you are still left with an inner
freedom—a dignity and a defiance in the human spirit. As
Mahatma Gandhi told his followers at an historic meeting
in Bombay on 8 August 1942, in the midst of the Indian
freedom struggle: 'The bond of the slave is snapped the
moment he considers himself to be a free being.'

In his book *Out of the evil night* (1959), the Norwegian
resistance fighter Leif Hovelsen tells how he was liberated
from the lust for revenge against the Gestapo officer who
had tortured him. During his capture, and threatened with
execution, Hovelsen was offered his freedom if he would
betray his friends in the resistance. 'I felt in my heart there
was no other option than a clear "No",' Hovelsen wrote.
'As I was about to take this deep resolve, something
extraordinary took place. I experienced the contradiction of

being truly free at the unique point of having lost everything.' Hovelsen survived the war and went on to be a powerful advocate of reconciliation in post-war Europe (Obituary, *Daily Telegraph*, 24 October 2011).

The kingdom of God, then, is within as well as being the ideal notion for the world's power structures. Those in the commanding heights of the world's political and economic power still need to acknowledge the words which often conclude the Lord's Prayer: *Thine is the kingdom, the power and the glory*. Obviously, the coming of the kingdom of God is still a work in progress, 2,000 years after Christ first gave us his prayer.

It has been said that the world is getting better and the world is getting worse at the same time—reflecting a cosmic struggle for the soul of humanity. Communications technology, the media and the Internet have brought the world much closer to a single whole, the so-called 'global village'. And social media sparked revolutions in the Arab world and elsewhere. But the abuse of technology contributed towards making the 20th Century the most barbaric and violent in human history. How, then, can we possibly say, 'Thy Kingdom come'? Each generation has to discover for itself what 'Thy Kingdom come' really means for them.

What it meant for the Israelites, the Jewish people, at the time of King Herod and Jesus, was far different from what they imagined. For Jesus decisively rejected earthly power during his temptations in the wilderness (Luke 4, vv 1-13) and declared that the kingdom of God was not of this world, in the sense of earthly power. Rather, the clue to building the kingdom of God lies in the next key phrase of Jesus' great prayer.

QUESTIONS:
Where is God's kingdom?
Why hasn't it come already?
*What can I do to make it real in my own life? In the lives
    of others? In the world as a whole?*

5. Thy will be done on Earth as it is in heaven

IF GOD'S KINGDOM is to come, and his will to be done on Earth, then the implication is that we need to dethrone what we honour in his place. What kingdoms do we enthrone in our lives in place of God's will? Or to put it another way, what is our first love? Money? Ambition? Fame? Power? Control? Revenge? Sex? The good life? Comfort and ease? Some of these have a legitimate place in our lives in the right context. But they all need to be sublimated to the greater will of God, in whose will lies our perfect freedom and happiness. As Jesus says, 'I have come in order that you might have life—life in all its fullness' (John 10, v 10, GNT). The North African saint, Augustine of Hippo, said, 'Our hearts are restless till they find their rest in thee.' Or as Archbishop François Fenelon put it: 'The peace of the soul consists in an absolute resignation to the will of God.'

It sounds like the very denial of freedom and personality. We want to 'be ourselves', to find fulfilment. Yet if we are created in God's image and likeness, so also in his will lies the flowering of our personalities, our greatest potential and fulfilment. As a teenager I had no trouble in accepting the notion that, if we and the entire universe are all created by an intelligence we call God—the alternative that we and the entire universe are simply an accident seemed too preposterous to be believable—then it made logical sense to believe, and accept, that God's will for our lives, the divine purpose for each of us on Earth, is the most fulfilling one possible.*

It would be far greater than anything we could conjure up for ourselves in the pursuit of our own self-will. But I found that it took a radical change of heart for this theoretical position to become something of a reality in my life.

Thy will be done on Earth as it is in heaven is the very heart of the Lord's Prayer. 'It is,' says Roger Hicks, 'a revolutionary programme that has often been turned into a pious drone' (*The Lords Prayer and modern man,* 1967). We say it without reflecting on its far-reaching implications. But how is it to come about? Notice the phrase 'on Earth'. Not just in my back yard, or my community, or my country, but on the entire Earth. In the original Greek, the word actually used translates as 'cosmos', not just the Earth but the entire universe.

This, then, is a challenge to human power structures with all their fallibility, whether governments, international organizations, Churches or religious organizations.

The way for God's will be to be done on Earth is for it to be done in the sum total of all of our lives individually. Were that to be achieved then we would have created, or God would have allowed us to create, heaven on Earth. It represents an ideal vision rather than an immediate reality, even if we try to make it a reality in our individual lives. A British prime minister once said, on coming to office, that he

---

*To those who would denigrate religious belief, Rabbi Jonathan Wittenberg of the New North London Synagogue gives a robust defence of the role of religion: 'It would be wrong to demonize religion or marginalize its contribution in the public square. Religious communities have much to give and secular society needs their contribution. Respect for God's Earth, reverence for life, the centrality of community and responsibility, the passion for social justice, the primacy of compassion, the search for wisdom, the awareness that we are accountable for all our actions, these too are irreplaceable values in any society.' (Credo column, *The Times,* 31 March 2012.)

wanted to see 'a nation at ease with itself'. I reflected at the time, that the only way for this really to happen is for each of us individually to be at peace with our consciences.

Frank Buchman, the American Lutheran pastor who founded the Moral Re-Armament movement, said on his deathbed in 1960, 'I want to see the world governed by people who are governed by God.' Is this an argument for a theocracy? Perhaps not, and certainly not in the sense of the rule of law decided by religious institutions. And, anyway, who is to say whether or not any particular civil leader has a direct personal connection with God, a precondition of a theocracy? But perhaps Buchman's call was more in line with the more literal meaning of theo-cracy—the sense of God's internal rule of the heart in individuals, including those who are in the corridors of power.

It could be said that God's will is *being* done on Earth whenever it is done in the life of a single individual. This is obviously not the completion of God's will on earth. But as the Russian writer Alexander Solzhenitsyn said, 'One word of truth outweighs the world.'* So we could perhaps equally say, 'One person whose will is wholly given to God outweighs the world.' Or as Buchman used to quote, 'The world has yet to see what God can do in, by and through one person who is wholly given to Him.'

What does it mean for God's will to be done in one's life? We can never wholly know, and it would be arrogant to assume that God's will is wholly done in my or anyone else's life. But we can have the *intention*, the set of the will. And then, perhaps occasionally, God's will, God's grace, can act through us.

---

*See the film *One Word of Truth*, Anglo-Nordic Productions Trust (1981), based on Solzhenitsyn's acceptance text for his Nobel Prize for Literature, 1970.

When I was 19 I spent a week at a conference organized by Moral Re-Armament* in the north of England. I had the good fortune to sit at lunch opposite Patrick, an Oxford graduate, whom I had never met before. He asked me some pertinent questions. Had I measured the conduct of my life in the light of Christ's absolute claims on my life? Had I put right anything that was wrong in my life that did not measure up to four moral standards: honesty, purity of heart, unselfishness and love for people?

I might have taken offence at such directness from a total stranger. For others, such 'soul surgery' would have required 'intelligent restraint and nonchalant reserve', as Buchman put it. But perhaps the grace of God was at work in Patrick. Perhaps he had noticed a particular need in me. Somehow his questions came at a time when I was open and ready to receive them. I was searching for the next step in my life and was aware of my moral compromises, particularly in relation to a girlfriend whom I had no intention of marrying. Patrick urged me to reflect on my life in the light of the four moral virtues and—here was the sting—to chat with him again in a few days.

So, a few days later we went out in his car. He pulled over in a narrow lane with a glorious view towards the Welsh mountains. We sat quietly for a few moments.

'So what thoughts did you get?' he asked.

'Oh, just to stop biting my fingernails,' I replied.

'Is that all? I'm sure there's more to it than that. Let's have another time of quiet.'

I knew I needed to come clean with him about what was really troubling me—my relationship with my girlfriend whom I had been seeing for three years though I never really felt that we were meant for each other. I had wanted to break

---

*MRA, an international movement founded before the outbreak of World War II, now known as Initiatives of Change.

it off but hadn't known how to without hurting her feelings. I had two clear thoughts in that time of silent reflection: 'Break off the relationship; and tell my parents what I have been getting up to which they may or may not know about.'

With sensitivity Patrick got me to tell him the kind of things I had been getting up to. It made me feel ashamed— no bad thing—and gave me a sense of a reawakened conscience. Then he said something which took me completely by surprise: 'Would you like to give your life to God?' He meant, was I willing to commit my will to God's will and ways for my life insofar as I could understand them?

I had no idea what this would mean in practice. But I felt as though I was standing on the top of a diving board, and needed to take the plunge. So to my own surprise I said yes. I had an inkling that if I didn't take this plunge I would never know what I would be missing. And so I found myself saying a prayer. At first there was a long silence. 'Are you scared?' Patrick asked. No, but I wasn't sure what I was supposed to say. Then I simply made a declaration to God in front of this witness, Patrick: 'Dear God, I give my life to you.' It was an unemotional statement of intention and will. Yet as soon as I had said it I had a great sense of relief and inner liberation; a sense that it no longer mattered what others might think of me. I was free to be my own man as God showed me. Free to do his will, in the faith that his plan and purpose for my life would be far more fulfilling and satisfying than anything I could make up for myself under my own steam.

I returned home to tell the girl we should break it off. She was hysterical, crying uncontrollably, as she had hoped we would spend the summer together. It dawned on me just how selfish and self-centred I had been. Yet I knew that without making this break I would not be free to find my true calling and destiny—and probably not she either. We would have held each other back. Years later I was walking up Fleet Street in London when I ran into her father. It was a chance for me to acknowledge that I had treated his daughter badly. 'Oh, don't worry,' he replied, 'She's happily married and had a child.' It was something of a relief to me.

I meanwhile found my calling in life through journalism, writing, editing and publishing, particularly on behalf of Initiatives of Change. I never dreamt, at the time of that decisive prayer, that this would be the case. Nor that I would also go on to have a life-long involvement with India where I was to work for several years. Thanks to all this I also met my wife, Jan, as we worked together on publications in London.

The great Scottish theologian Henry Drummond (1851-1897) had a helpful take on 'how to find the will of God':

1. Pray;

2. Think;

3. Talk to wise people, but do not regard their decision as final;

4. Beware of the bias of your own will, but do not be too much afraid of it. God never unnecessarily thwarts your nature and likings. It is a mistake to think that His will is in the line with the disagreeable;

5. Meantime do the next thing. Doing God's will in small things is the best preparation for doing it in great things;

6. When decision and action are necessary, go ahead;

7. Never reconsider the decision when it is finally acted upon;

8. And you will probably not find out till afterwards, perhaps long afterwards, that you have been led at all!

None of this is a recipe for an easy life. We are not called to comfort and ease so much as to fulfillment. Nor are we spared pain and suffering, which are part and parcel of life. We all suffer loss and bereavement, whether through illness, old age or in tragic circumstances. Nor can we always protect others from the deep pain that the world inflicts on them. Doing God's will sometimes involves tough decisions. After all, it cost Christ the ultimate sacrifice: his crucifixion on the Cross. He's been there; done that. He knows what we go through. Sharing in the suffering of the world deepens our sense of empathy, our compassion, for the deep suffering of others in an unredeemed world.

We can speculate as to what it would really mean for God's will to be done on Earth as it is in heaven. What would it mean for poverty reduction? The environment? Climate change? The global economy? Eradication of disease? Family life and relationships? Interfaith relationships and the partnership of civilizations? Could we see the birth of the 'civilization of love' that Pope John Paul II talked about? James Jones, the Bishop of Liverpool, writes: 'The doing of God's will on Earth as it is done in heaven requires us to challenge unjust structures, political and economic, and to insist on fair trade and sustainable methods of food and fuel production. The earthing of heaven requires it.' (*Jesus and the Earth*, 2003)

One thing is clear: there is a choice for each of us, between materialism and hedonism or spiritual values and ultimately the will of God, a choice which determines not just our personal survival but also the survival of the planet. If we believe that God is the 'alpha and omega', the A-Z, personified in Jesus Christ (Revelation 1, v 8; Revelation 22, v 13), when we pray 'Thy kingdom come; Thy will be done on Earth as it is in heaven', what in effect we are saying is, 'God, touch my life; and don't just be a part of my life but be the central motivation of my life. Help me to find your calling for my life.' Nothing else, no other relationship, is as important.

QUESTIONS:
What does it mean to do God's will?
What are the implications?
What needs to change in my life?
What needs to change in the world?
Do things change gradually or do they change radically?
How do we each find our calling in life?

6. Give us this day our daily bread

SO FAR, the focus of the great prayer has been on God and his purposes; his expectations of and for us. Now the focus turns to our needs if we are to fulfill his purposes for our lives and for the world. The spotlight shifts from *Thy* to *us*. *How* are we to fulfill his will for our lives? What do we need?

Well, first of all, we need daily bread. This sounds, at first, like a simple request for food—our material need. And at one level it is exactly that. Bread—or, perhaps more likely today, rice or pasta or *chapatti*—is basic to our diet and keeps us alive. It did so for the Israelites as they escaped from captivity in Egypt towards the land that God promised to them in the East. As they cross the 'wilderness' or desert, by the middle of the third month of their great trek they are beginning to starve. At this point, God promises to rain down bread from heaven—but only enough for each day's supply. In the early morning dew, fine flakes appear on the ground—'fine as hoar-frost'. As the Israelites gather this 'manna from heaven' they share it between them. It was, says the writer of the story, 'white, like coriander seed, and it tasted like a wafer made with honey'. Astonishingly, it kept them supplied for the next 40 years until they arrived in the Promised Land where they could settle. It is an extraordinarily vivid story (Exodus, 16).

So, we pray for our material needs. God's provision is revisited in the story of Jesus feeding the 5,000 people who have been listening to him out in the desert, as night begins to fall. How are we to feed all these people, the disciples ask him. They have between them only five barley loaves and two small fish. Jesus consecrates, or blesses, the food and gives it to the disciples to distribute. By the time they have all had enough, the disciples gather up 12 baskets of the scraps, the leftovers (Mark 6, vv 30-44). Later Jesus feeds 4,000 people and seven baskets of scraps are collected (Mark 8, vv 1-9).

God is not disinterested in the care of our bodies any less than the care of our souls.

We are left to ponder on how large a global population it is possible to sustain within the earth's finite resources. Does God know our needs sufficiently to feed a world population likely to peak at 12 billion, according to scientists' best forecasts? And in the words of a song by musician Kathleen Dodds, 'Are people a problem or an answer?' Can we collectively, and unselfishly, meet the world's material needs at a time of escalating population growth, finite resources and climate change? Can we care enough to share enough?

There is, of course, much more to this part of the Lord's Prayer than just our material needs. More fundamentally it addresses our spiritual need for the presence of God in our lives. And Jesus himself is the bread of life. He tells the crowd that follows him around the Lake of Galilee: 'I tell you the truth, it is not Moses who has given you the bread from heaven, but it is my Father who gives you the true bread from heaven. For the bread of God is he who comes down from heaven and gives life to the world.' He goes on to say: 'I am the bread of life. He who comes to me will never go hungry, and he who believes in me will never be thirsty.' (John 6, vv 31-35, NIV).

In the dramatic climax to Jesus' life on Earth, leading to his crucifixion, he shares a final meal with his closest colleagues in a secret location in Jerusalem, an upstairs room in a supporter's house, as he anticipates his arrest by the authorities. In that 'last supper', marking the Jewish Passover meal, he breaks unleavened bread and passes it to his disciples. He tells them that the bread is his body and that whenever they eat it in future they should do so in remembrance of him. Likewise, the wine which they share is a symbol of his blood which he is about to shed as he is crucified on a cross. (Matthew 26, vv 17-30; Mark 14, vv 12-26; Luke 22, vv 7-23.) The bread and wine have been formalized in church services as the Eucharist, taken during Mass or Holy Communion. By so doing, we are 'feeding' on the memory of Jesus and all that he stands for and means to us. But Jesus also seems to say that *whenever* we meet together over a meal we should do so in remembrance of him. We reverence the food that we eat in thanks for God's provision. And we feed in our spirit on the sacrifice of Jesus, who by facing the cross bore the burden of the world's violence and sins and shared in the pain of the world.

When Jesus says 'Give us this day our daily bread', he hints at the fact that we shall need to feed on the memory and living presence of him each day. We feed on him, as it were. We cannot do anything worthwhile without him. 'Our daily bread' literally and metaphorically means Jesus himself. We need to renew the contract with him every day. As Monsignor Roderick Strange, Rector of the Pontifical Beda College in Rome, writes in *The Times* (Credo column, 8 August 2009), 'Those who have eaten manna in the wilderness have died, but this bread which He identifies as Himself, is the new bread that nourishes for eternal life. It is those who have faith in Him who will find their deepest desires satisfied and their thirsts slaked.'

Indeed, as Canon David Watson points out, in the gospel feast, 'the menu is superlative—"the peace which transcends all understanding", Philippians 4, v 7; "inexpressible and glorious joy", 1 Peter 1, v 8; "love that surpasses knowledge", Ephesians 3, v 19; "total forgiveness", 1 John 1, v 9;

"life to the full", John 10, v 10; and "glorious freedom", Romans 8, v 20, among other things. Ever since the death and resurrection of Jesus, the gospel feast has been ready and God has been saying "Come".'

Reflecting on this further, we are left to ask ourselves what do we feed on if it is not the presence of God in our lives? Where do we search for satisfaction and peace of heart? In money, possessions, food, drink, human relationships, sex, power, ambition, fame, success, revenge? Some of these are good and necessities in the right context; some not. But none are ends in themselves. All are transitory. And we can create false gods out of insatiable desires, from binge drinking to 'retail therapy'. Food, for instance, is necessary for our survival, but gorging ourselves may reflect a deeper dissatisfaction in life.

So how do we feed on this 'bread of life' which Jesus identifies as himself? By reading the scriptures, by prayer and worship, by taking part in the Eucharist, and also by taking time out each day for silent reflection—to allow the whispers of the Holy Spirit to touch our lives, to feed our spirits, to give us inspiration. For many around the world this is a daily practice and reality. It fills us with gratitude for God's good gifts to us and strengthens us for the tasks at hand.*

Finally, why does Jesus say, 'Give us *this day* our daily bread'? Why not *this week*? Or, indeed, for our entire life? Why can't we swallow it whole, as it were? Why can't we have it all? Well, perhaps Jesus is simply being realistic. There is only so much we can cope with. 'Sufficient unto the day is the evil thereof' (Matthew 6, v 34, KJB) or 'Each day

---

*See the booklet *The Sound of Silence*, Caux Books, ISBN 978-1-56592-479-6, in which I suggest that the inspiration which comes in silent reflection acts as both an anchor in life and a springboard to action: www.soundofsilence.org

has enough trouble of its own' (NIV). So each day is a fresh start, a chance to begin all over again. We need to renew the contract, renew our deep personal friendship with God each day—and especially as the day begins. We can take time for quiet prayer and reflection; to create our early morning 'space for grace', to realize and renew our utter dependence on the grace of God for the day ahead, remembering that he is our daily bread. And in doing so we don't need to be gripped by fear of what the future might or might not hold. Indeed, 'Fear not' is one of Jesus' most repeated phrases in the gospels. As the words of John Henry Newman's hymn *Lead kindly light* say: 'I do not ask to see the distant scene; one step enough for me.' Or as John Hughes' Welsh hymn *Cwm Rhondda* says: 'bread of heaven, feed me now and evermore'.

QUESTIONS:
What do I most need in my life? Materially? Spiritually?
Where do I find my sources of satisfaction?
Are they the right ones?
What are God's instructions for me for today?

7. Forgive us our trespasses as we forgive those who trespass against us

Now the bar is raised. The challenge gets greater. Some see forgiveness as a weakness and a betrayal. They would rather have vengeance or retribution, often driven by bitterness and hate—an eye for an eye and a tooth for a tooth, though even this was intended, in its original Hebrew context, as a *limitation* within the notion of justice in order to prevent an escalation of retribution.

Others see forgiveness as a strength and a liberation—a letting go of past wrongs; a freeing from the burden of guilt, without which our sins would simply go on accumulating to become an unbearable load. As Psalm 32 says:

Blessed is he whose transgressions are forgiven, whose sins are covered.
Blessed is the man whose sin the Lord does not count against him and in whose spirit is no deceit....
Then I acknowledged my sin to you and did not cover up my iniquity.
I said, 'I will confess my transgressions to the Lord'—
And you forgave the guilt of my sin.' (NIV, vv 1-2, 5)

Billy Graham said, 'Perhaps the most glorious word in the English language is forgiveness.' The American author Philip Yancy, in his book *What's so amazing about grace?*, describes forgiveness as 'the last best word in the English language'. 'Forgiveness alone can alter the cycle of blame and pain, breaking the chain of ungrace,' he writes. 'Forgiveness offers a way out. It does not settle all the questions of blame and fairness—often it pointedly evades those questions—but it does allow a relationship to start over.'

There is a profound humility in 'Forgive us our trespasses'—it suggests a recognition of our wrongs; an admission that they exist. It is the very antithesis of the pride that knows no wrong, the deadliest of the deadly sins. Yancy quotes Lewis Smeede of Fuller Theological Seminary: 'The first, and often the only, person to be healed by forgiveness is the person who does the forgiveness. When we genuinely forgive, we set a prisoner free and then discover that the prisoner we set free was us.' 'Not to forgive,' Yancy comments, 'imprisons me in the past and locks out all potential for change.'

Julian Bond, Director of the Christian Muslim Forum of Britain, points out that forgiveness is 'conditional and reciprocal'.* 'Forgive us our trespasses *as* we forgive those who trespass against us.' The meaning in English is double-edged. The 'as' can be understood simply to imply *similar to* or it can mean *because* or *when* we forgive those who have offended us, which is far more consequential. Whichever way we take it, we also have to forgive as well as accept forgiveness.

Indeed, Jesus takes it further when he tells his disciples after his resurrection: 'If you forgive anyone his sins, they are forgiven; if you do not forgive them, they are not forgiven' (John 20, v 23, NIV). Other people *depend* on our forgiveness. Elsewhere he tells the disciple Simon Peter: 'whatever you bind on earth will be bound in heaven, and whatever you loose on earth will be loosed in heaven.'

---

*Julian Bond said this at the launch of the book *No enemy to conquer: forgiveness in an unforgiving world* by Michael Henderson, at the St Ethelburga's Centre for Reconciliation and Peace, London, 13 May 2009. Henderson has written several excellent books on forgiveness, including *Forgiveness: breaking the chain of hate* and *The forgiveness factor*. See his website at: www.mh.iofc.org

(Matthew 16, v 19, NIV). Heaven, it seems, remains to a certain extent in our hands. The point is that we have the choice to forgive and if we don't forgive others, who may need our forgiveness, they remain outside our forgiveness in our own hearts, and indeed may even become our victims as much as we are theirs.

Whichever way we see it, there also needs to be admission of guilt on our part in the first place, rather than pointing the finger of blame at others. The Burmese educationist Daw Nien Tha used to say, 'When I point my finger at my neighbour, there are three more fingers pointing back at me.'

Monsignor Roderick Strange points out that 'Our weaknesses, our flaws, the fault-lines in our character are a part of us. They are not irremediable, but they are there and they cannot be overcome by an apology alone, however heartfelt, or a change of heart. We have to work to overcome them and we may struggle to do so throughout our lives. That is why forgiveness, fortunately for us, is unlimited.' How many of us are aware of an abiding weakness, an Achilles' heel, in our lives that continues to dog us and which only the grace of God can deal with?

Monsignor Strange goes on to say that, for forgiveness to become real, 'it still requires the sorrow that leads to a change of heart and a readiness to acknowledge our faults, and the determination, so far as it lies in our power, not to repeat them in future. Those are the conditions that make forgiveness real. Forgiveness is unlimited, but it is not unconditional.' (Credo, *The Times*, 9 September 2011)

So forgiveness is a tall order. Yet it has been offered, and accepted, in the most extreme of circumstances. How can someone who has lost a loved one to murder or been the victim of rape or a brutal regime ever possibly countenance the notion of forgiveness? It sounds impossible to contemplate. Jesus himself was persecuted and died through the brutality of others. He identifies with our suffering through his own experience. Yet even at the moment of his greatest agony, as he hangs dying on the Cross he says, 'Forgive them, Lord, for they know not what they do.'

In far less dramatic circumstances, the smallest slight can lead to a resentment that lingers on and assumes enormous proportions, poisoning our minds and memories. A character in the multimedia drama about forgiveness *Consider this...* by Jack Lynch (Lynchpin Productions Theatre Company, 2012) says: 'It is the ant, not the elephant, the raspberry seed not the the coconut that gets in our way.' As the Fleet Street journalist and playwright Peter Howard graphically put it: 'The bottom has a longer memory than the boot.'

In his book *God at work* (2007), the banker Ken Costa tells of an incident in his business life which makes him suggest that we don't call on this prayer nearly enough:

> On one occasion, a colleague was not straight with me, and I subsequently found out from others about his bad-mouthing me. I was furious. Half of me wanted nothing more to do with him; half of me knew that we had to work together under one roof and therefore we had to talk. To be honest, I never wanted to trust him again. But we are created in God's image. The certainty and ferocity of self-righteous outpourings when we are hurt bend to the persistent but much more tentative prod-dings of conscience. In these circumstances we should take the first step, even if we do so gingerly. After all, it's a very raw nerve that is touched. There is nothing wrong with being wary—but wariness should not replace the willingness to build a new relationship. Reconciliation is at the heart of faith and this pushes us, usually against our natural instincts, to begin to rebuild trust. And God who is trustworthy teaches us to trust again.

But how do we start to put things right? Step one is the desire to set matters straight. Here too we know that

God inclines our hearts towards reconciliation, so that even if we do not feel inclined to make peace we can ask him to give us the grace to do so. Thereafter an approach needs to be made. In my case this was a short handwritten letter—email is too often the vehicle for quick rage. Then there should be frank discussion. There is no lasting value in not being up front about the facts. Expect a response—even a vigorous one. After all, the accusations that one makes regarding a breaking of trust go to the essence of any person's self-esteem. After the meeting there is not an automatic reset to the status quo ante. That takes time, but our behaviour has to reflect the reality that we have totally forgiven that person. I hope that I did so and that he knew that no grudges were kept.

The 'Our Father' is invaluable for this reason: 'Forgive us our shortfalls as we forgive those who have wronged us.' We forgive as we have been forgiven. We say this prayer not nearly enough. It is truly the manifesto of the person at work. Thus invoked, an energy that comes from outside our own being enables us to walk in the freedom of new trust. Yes, there will be an accusation of naivety. 'Don't trust others' is after all a slogan for many who have been hurt at work. Sometimes we have to live with the consequences of trusting too readily. That could be part of our calling to suffer with Christ.

A retired publishing executive and editor, John Munro, writes in his memoirs *Calm before Coffee* (2012) how this section of Lord's Prayer prompted him to think of his estranged mother and to seek reconciliation with her. She had been unable to care for him after he was born and had to arrange private placements, a children's home and foster parents. When he was 14 his foster mother persuaded him to break off all contact with his birth mother. It wasn't until ten years later, after he began to find a faith and recite this prayer, that he realised he needed to ask her forgiveness for the resentment that her had harboured against her. His moving book tells the unfolding story of his coming to terms with his insecure childhood and finding healing, faith and a sense of purpose in life.

Let me also divert to my personal experience for a moment. It may be a mistake to draw universal truth from individual experience—everyone's are different. However some common lessons can perhaps be learnt. On the whole I had a warm relationship with my father. I never knew him to lose his temper. He was sacrificially generous to me during my school education, encouraging me to stay an extra year at school to take a third A level exam. (It was years later that I fully appreciated the financial sacrifice he made on my behalf.)

I remember once having to make an important decision about my future career path. I had an inkling of what it should be and had written down my thoughts in a time of silent reflection. I phoned my father to share them with him. To my astonishment, he told me that he had had the same thoughts, which he read out to me, almost exactly word for word as mine. It was a huge encouragement and I remember putting the phone down and laughing. It was a great relief to have that confirmation and I was put completely at peace of heart in making the decision.

But there was one incident between us later on which left a scar on my memory, and which resurfaced in my thinking and emotions long after he died. It focussed around his will for another decision in my life he had wanted me to take. Instead of talking to me about this personally and privately, it arose in a conversation with someone else at which I was present. My father expressed his will for me to this third person in front of me without having talked it through with me first. It came as a complete shock to me. No doubt my father meant well. But the way he did this upset me. It was to have repercussions on my relationships with others—because, trusting his judgment, I took up his suggestion. Yet, at the same time, I could never be really sure if it was God's will for me, or simply my father's. Could I really trust his judgment, or even my own, in this particular matter?

It was not till some years after he had died that I realized how angry I was about it. Whenever things appeared to go wrong, it was easy to blame my father instead of my own decision-making. Yet there seemed to be nothing I could do to heal my anger towards him, which occasionally surfaced in other family relationships. It may even have played a part in my later developing a heart condition for which I needed an operation. They say that there is nothing better for the health of the heart than fun and laughter, as well as good exercise. Anger can have the opposite effect.

Then, one day, I had the unexpected thought to pray for my father, now long dead. We are encouraged to 'pray for the souls of the faithfully departed'. That night, after I had prayed for him and his memory, I dreamt that I was with him. We were laughing together. We laughed so much that I must have laughed out loud in my sleep, for my laughter woke me up. It was an extraordinary experience. From then on I felt that my father had gone on to a good place. I could never feel the same anger towards him again. This didn't prevent me from still being tempted towards anger or bitterness. But it took away its sting. Moreover, the more I reflected on this experience the more I realized that I too had been wrong. My bitterness was wrong. The point was that I need not have chosen to follow my father's suggestion, however good or wrong it may have seemed. The choice was still mine, and I had no right, let alone need, to be angry against him. I may never fully know if my father's will for me was right or not, and it probably doesn't matter anyway as all our decisions can be redeemed by God and his forgiveness.

Do we ever blame God for our decisions in life that we feel are taken in obedience to his will and which don't always seem to work out? How much do we recognize that God, in his infinite wisdom, has given us free will to choose to obey him or not? Is it fair to blame God for things that don't always work out the way we expect in life? There is also the matter of our personal responsibility for our own decision-making. Yet we can trust God to have our best interests for a most fulfilling life at heart. It is worth remembering that every generation has something for which they need to forgive their forebears, if we are to sever the umbilical cord of anger, bitterness and hatred that ties us to the past rather than liberating us towards a better future.

QUESTIONS:
What do I need forgiveness for in my life?
What fault-lines in my character need to change?
Who do I need to forgive?
What steps can I take?

8. Lead us not into temptation...

THIS, AT FIRST, appears to be nonsense. Why on earth would God want to lead us into temptation anyway? Surely, his job is to lead us away from temptation and to protect us from evil, not to lead us towards it. So why should we need to pray for God not to lead us into temptation? He doesn't play games with us, surely. So what is the real meaning of this sentence? It has been said that it actually means 'Don't put us to the test.' As William Barclay points out: 'In its New Testament usage, to tempt people is not so much to seek to seduce them into sin as it is to test their strength and their loyalty and their ability for service.' He explains that the verb *peirazein* used for 'tempt' in the Bible is often better translated by the word 'test'. 'Here then,' Barclay continues, 'is one of the great and precious truths about temptation. Temptation is not designed to make us fall. Temptation is designed to make us stronger and better men and women. Temptation is not designed to make us sinners. It is designed to make us good.' So we should welcome our temptations as a test of our strength.

Jesus, of course, knows what it is like and shares the experience with us. He was put to the test and came through the ordeal. He faced the strongest temptations towards materialism, the dramatic gesture and earthly power, as he contemplated his mission during 40 days in the Wilderness. In the Garden of Gethsemane he prayed that he would not have to drink the 'cup', the poisoned chalice as it were, of God's will for him. He knew it would lead to his arrest, flogging, prosecution on trumped up charges, humiliation, crucifixion, death and ultimate resurrection. But he knew he had to go through with it nonetheless. He told his disciples gathered with him at that darkest of moments in human history, when the forces of evil were ranged against the Son of Man—the Son of God—himself, to persist in prayer in order to resist the full force of temptation that was about to be unleashed—the temptation to violence and to the denial of friendship with Jesus, about to be suffered by Simon Peter.

So this is a compassionate line in the Lord's Prayer: we should not have to go through what Jesus himself went through. He has carried the Cross for us; borne the burden of our sins. And in so far as we share the burden of the Cross with him, we do so by the crossing out of our own self-will and choosing to follow God's will in our daily lives: the big self-centred 'I' of self-will is crossed out by the 'Thou' of God's will.

Nonetheless, it is instructive to reflect on where our temptations lie, in order to be aware of them and move away from them. They may well rest in any one, or combination of, the seven deadly sins, or Cardinal Vices: wrath, greed, sloth, pride (in the sense of hubris), lust, envy and gluttony. Then there are also the temptations of power and control, about which more later.

Of the cardinal vices, pride is the most ambiguous, and sometimes the most deadly. It has both a positive and negative connotation. In some church and spiritual traditions pride was what cast the Devil out of heaven: his ambition to usurp the place of God. Pride is what prevents me from being honest with my wife when I've made a mistake or done something stupid. So pride is what makes me want to cover up instead of come clean. Pride says, 'Isn't my fault', when perhaps it is. Pride can be the opposite of humility. 'Pride,' says John Barnett, founder of the Discover the Book Ministries in Oklahoma, 'is the sin of competing with God... it makes you self-reliant, self-absorbed, self-deceived, self-confident, self-conscious, self-sufficient, self-satisfied, self-focused, self-centred and self-driven. It makes you unreliable because nobody can tell you what to do... unloving, because you won't sacrifice for others... un-teachable, because nobody can correct you.' (Quoted in *The Word for Today*, UCB, 23 January 2011).

On the other hand, Stephen Cherry offers the opposite in his 10 disciplines for Lent, published in *Reform* magazine (March 2011), following his book *Barefoot disciple: walking the way of passionate humility* (2010):

1. Take off your shoes; 2. Admit a recent mistake;
3. Pocket an insult; 4. Behave as a child; 5. Step across a boundary; 6. Give up grumbling; 7. Practise hospitality;
8. Do something for someone else; 9. Be proud of yourself; 10. Encourage others.

'While bad pride is to be avoided,' he writes in relation to point 9, 'there is such a thing as good pride. It is a very down to earth feeling and we have it when we allow ourselves to look at work well done with kind and straightforward eyes. It is child-like to have good pride, because there is nothing arrogant or conceited in it. Good pride accepts praise gratefully but humbly and allows you to recognize that your efforts are worthwhile and achievements valid. Good pride is not pushy and might be expressed modestly. It is a good feeling and not only consistent with healthy humility—but a sign of it. Meanwhile, try to shake off all forms of bad pride: arrogance, conceitedness and chauvinism, and do away with false modesty. No more "little me", thank you.'

We are reminded of St Paul's great hymn to love: 'Love is patient, love is kind. It does not envy, it does not boast, it is not proud. It is not rude, it is not self-seeking, it is not easily angered, it keeps no scores of wrongs. Love does not delight in evil but rejoices with the truth. It always protects, always trusts, always hopes, always perseveres.' (1 Corinthians 13, vv 4-7, NIV). The King James Version of the Bible puts it far more colourfully: '...Charity vaunteth not itself, is not puffed up.'

So it is well worth remembering the counterpoints of the seven deadly sins: patience, charity, diligence, humility, chastity, kindness and temperance. Plato also listed the four cardinal virtues as prudence, justice, temperance (or restraint) and fortitude (or courage), subsequently emphasized by Thomas Aquinas in his *Summa Theologica*.

Temptation is, of course, different from succumbing. As Frank Buchman said, 'You can't stop crows flying over your head; but you can stop them nesting in your hair!' Hardly a likely scenario. But it makes the point that temptation will always be there. And we can be aware of our most persistent temptations—as well as our unexpected ones. We don't have to succumb to them. In fact, through resisting temptations we find strength of character and growth of personality. In succumbing to them we diminish ourselves and let others down. We should, at any rate, regard our temptations as a compliment: they are a sign that evil, personified in the Devil, is sufficiently concerned about our redemptive state to want to undermine it, to blunt our best efforts. We must be doing something right if the Devil is that concerned!

I find that, no matter what my age, my temptations are boringly repetitive and persistent. They don't get any less the older one gets. Our temptations, if honestly admitted, can be a link across the generations. If the older generation is honest and open enough, their temptations can be a source of empathy towards the young—and a source of fascination for them. 'Hey, Dad, are you like that too?' 'Dad, what did you get up to when you were young?'

Temptations' persistence is perhaps not surprising, as temptations which are dwelt on can become hard-wired into the synapses of the brain. They remain attractive, however much they are dross dressed up as gold.

So how to deal with temptation? It has been well said that the melancholy sequence of 'the look, the thought, the fascination and the fall' needs to be broken between the first two and decisively between the second and the third. Easier said than done. But we should also remember the sequence: 'Sow a habit, reap a character; sow a character, reap a destiny.' This applies for good or ill, and the sum total of all our habits can also be reflected in our national characteristics. Of course there is the simple expedient: if one's temptation is to fall off cliffs, don't walk near the edge.

St Paul has encouraging words for us. In his first letter to the Corinthians he writes: 'No temptation has come our way that is too harsh for flesh and blood to bear. But God can be trusted not to allow you to suffer beyond your powers of endurance. He will see to it that temptation has its way out, so that it will be possible for you to bear it.' (1 Corinthians 10, v 13).

Julian Baggini, editor of *The Philosopher's Magazine*, has an interesting take on all this, writing in *The Times* (23 December 2009). His article was in response to controversial advice given by a priest, Father Tim Jones, who said that in some circumstances shop lifting by the impoverished might be justified. Baggini writes:

> There may be times when desperate circumstances require us to disregard our usual moral norms. One example is Jean Valjean's stealing a loaf of bread in Victor Hugo's *Les Miserables*, which most readers do not see as a heinous crime but as a justifiable act of desperation. But it was precisely because it was an extreme case that we excuse Valjean.... Valjean's story also reminds us that actions have consequences for character. Over time he becomes an habitual thief, illustrating the lesson that the psychologist Philip Zimbardo learnt from decades of

studying why ordinary, decent people do wicked things. It's not like *Star Wars*, where people flip over to the dark side. The long journey of 1,000 sins starts with a single step. 'When you first take those small steps, it's hard to imagine the slippery slope,' he says.

It is not inevitable that when lines in the moral sand get eroded, it's only a matter of time before we end up in a moral desert. But human beings are brilliantly inventive self-justifiers and one-off utilitarian calculations are all too easy to rig. How many people start by convincing themselves that an innocent drink need not lead to an affair, and end up reassuring that what others don't know can't hurt them? There are unforeseen, if not unforeseeable, consequences of thinking too much about only the foreseen ones.... So breaking promises for a good consequence has the bad consequence of undermining the very practice of promise-keeping upon which much of our moral lives depends.'

Being good requires that we do not reduce all our decisions to crude calculations. Refusing to do wrong even when it has benefits is necessary if we are to retain our moral inteFgrity.

Like Jean Valjean, Judas was also a thief. He was known to steal from the disciples' common purse. But whereas Valjean found redemption, Judas's pride prevented him from doing so. After he had betrayed Jesus in exchange for 30 pieces of silver, he was so overwhelmed by the enormity of his crime that he hanged himself.

If overweening pride is the deadliest of sins, avarice—inordinate greed and the love of money—is a close run second. There are more references to money and its use for good or ill in the Bible than there are to sex. It was Judas's love of money that led to his betrayal of Christ and his subsequent crucifixion. Perhaps St Paul's insistence that the love of money is the root of 'all kinds of evil' was simply recognition that placing our faith in money—putting the profit motive above all else—is simply unsustainable. It is a false security. It enthrones material acquisition above the spiritual. It dethrones God in our lives.

In the business world, the temptation to enthrone the profit motive as king can have disastrous consequences, as happened in the financial crash of 2008 which, according to the World Bank, threw 100 million people into poverty. Gordon Brown described it, in his book *Beyond the crash* (2010), as 'the first crisis of globalization'. 'Markets need morals,' he concluded in the headline of his last chapter, while Prime Minister David Cameron told the 2009 World Economic Forum in Davos, 'It is time to place the market within a moral framework.'

Profit is of course a good thing, and banks at their best provide an essential social service. But the temptation is to make profit the primary motive. If a business person or a banker says that the primary purpose of business is to make money then the retort should be no, no, no. The primary purpose of business—including banking—is to provide the goods and services that people, communities and the wider world need; to meet human need, to give a living wage, and to raise the living standards of millions of human beings out of grinding poverty and into a basic standard of fairness and justice. Profit is a consequence of these motives and not an end in itself. As Tania Ellis writes in her book *The New Pioneers* (2010), we need a whole new paradigm for doing business in the world, based on corporate sustainability and responsibility and what is called 'triple bottom line' accounting which includes the welfare of people, planet and profit, in that order.

Ken Costa writes that 'the desire for more money has crippled many with so-called 'affluenza'—the disease that can't stop wanting more.' Indeed, the excessive pursuit of profit can have deadly consequences. When stock market or house price bubbles burst the losses can be so enormous that they lead to suicides.

Following the crash I wrote a Credo column in *The Times* (8 November 2008), under the headline 'The crisis of confidence ignites a crisis of conscience':

Never has a financial crisis focussed so starkly on moral, ethical and even spiritual issues. The words used by commentators have run the gamut of emotions: greed, dishonesty and fear, panic replacing confidence, risk and hubris versus prudence, and faith in the banking system or lack of it. Never have the virtues of trust and integrity been more needed in the global economy.

The whole edifice was built on maximizing profit, and a dishonest assessment of individual borrowers' credit-worthiness. It was bound to end in tears, and now millions pay the price in increased taxes and unemploy-ment. Despite the pain, it may all be healthy in the long run. The crisis is a chance to re-examine fundamental motives; and to ask how capitalism at its best is supposed to work. Where is our faith placed? In markets and profit? Or in something deeper?

Of course we all want our finances, including our pensions, to be in safe havens. We search for the best return on our assets. We move money around. Indeed there is a biblical precedent in Jesus's parable of the investment and return on talents. The one whose talents increased the most was most praised. The one who buried his talents in the ground (under the mattress?) was most condemned.

But those who are driven solely by the profit motive and 'the love of money', described by St Paul as 'the root of all evil', are discovering that security based on mate-rial wealth is an illusion. A curious weakness of human nature says that the more we have, the more we still want. When Rockefeller was asked 'How much is enough?' he is said to have replied, 'Just a little more'. Yet the roots of security and satisfaction lie elsewhere, not in amassing wealth but in seeking the divine purpose for our lives.

The crisis has called into question the whole capitalist system. Karl Marx's *Das Capital* has been flying off bookshelves. Could capitalism totally collapse, corrupted from within like the Roman Empire? Given that it is still the only show in town, how can capitalism be rescued from itself? To answer that question, we can turn to the father of capitalism himself.

We remember Adam Smith for his emphasis on the 'invisible hand' of the free market. If each person pursued their own interest, then the common good would also be served. But there was much more to it than that.

Smith was professor of moral philosophy at Glasgow University (1752-1764) and it was, he said, 'by far the most useful and therefore by far the happiest and most honourable period' of his life.

In 1759, 17 years before he published *The Wealth of Nations*, he wrote *The Theory of Moral Sentiments*. In it he referred to 'compassion, the emotion we feel for the misery of others'; and 'the Impartial Spectator' inside each of us which acted like 'a demi-god within the breast'. It was 'there to speak for itself and for others'. And 'in the race for wealth, if injustice is done, the Impartial Spectator changes sides'. In other words, greed and the profit motive could not be condoned if they led to injustice.

Moreover, Smith described the 'man within us'—in today's language the conscience—as 'the Vice-Regent of the Deity'; we needed to 'co-operate with the Deity and advance, as far as in our power, the plan of Providence'.

As Stephen Young, of the Caux Round Table group of

business executives, argues in his book *Moral Capitalism*, the separation of Smith's two texts has given us a distorted notion of how capitalism should work.

Capitalism cannot not be separated from conscience and even a divine providence, a guiding hand. For without conscience, without the 'invisible hand' of divine grace, untamed capitalism too easily leads to corruption—and to the greed and dishonesty, the loss of humanity and common sense, that we have seen in the financial markets. To rescue capitalism and the banking system, we need to revisit Adam Smith's moral philosophy—and our own consciences.

Then there is the temptation to power and control, whether by dictatorial regimes or in boardrooms. Whole populations, especially those in the Middle East, still live with the consequences of the abuse of power exerted by the British Empire, and before it the rapacious East India Company.*

Businessman David Erdal, a leading campaigner for employee owned companies, writes about the temptation of power and control in business, in his book *Beyond the corporation: humanity working* (2011):

'Many companies set out to create among their employees a feeling of ownership, without any real ownership. This can be done through team-building techniques, systems for making continuous improvement and through participative management styles. Managers themselves can be honest believers in these approaches. But the end result is deceitful: the employees feel like owners but have none of the rights and benefits of ownership. The psychological ownership that is induced is good for performance and good for the people

*See *The corporation that changed the world* by Nick Robins, Pluto Press, 2006.

involved, but it is false. It can be reversed overnight and the employees can do nothing about it.'

The alternative, he says, is to put ownership into the hands of the entire workforce, such as the John Lewis Partnership model, encouraging participation and a joint sense of responsibility towards one another. Erdal concludes:

> If financial ownership were used for the benefit of wide employee ownership rather than the self-enrichment of a few, what a difference that would make. The temptation will be to skew the ownership and power radically towards the senior people, the chief executive and directors who already do so well out of the current system. That has to be resisted. The powerful need a change of heart, to recognize that this is worth doing ... But the satisfactions to be gained from doing it are real and deep.

Professor Roger Steare of Cass Business School in the City of London told a forum in the London centre of Initiatives of Change, in November 2010, that 'the meaning of the word "economy" has been corrupted'. It used to mean 'less', 'thrift' or 'enough'. Now it had come to mean more. 'Whilst three per cent per annum GDP growth doesn't sound much, this means doubling the size of our economy every 20 years.' Our planetary resources were not only scarce but finite. 'If all seven billion of us were to live the American dream we'd need about four more planet Earths to sustain us.' We needed 'a fundamental reset in our understanding of economics, money and capitalism,' he said. Britain's economic wealth was 16 times what it was in 1950. 'But when two billion fellow beings live on less than $2 a day, I find it obscene for British citizens to talk about economic misery and material poverty.'

He continued: 'Our addiction to economic growth has created a poverty of the soul that is corrupting our family lives, our friendships and our communities. This philosophy of growth for its own sake is as addictive as tobacco, alcohol and crack cocaine. It is also just as deadly. We must again define economy as thrift and fairness—the moral virtues of temperance and justice.'

His research, with PricewaterhouseCoopers, into 'MoralDNA™' (www.MoralDNA.org), involving over 60,000 respondents from over 200 countries, has shown that three moral virtues define our moral character 'and save us from ourselves': 'Let us replace what Stephen Young (author of *Moral Capitalism*) calls "brute capitalism" with an ethos based on the universal moral values of wisdom, fairness and love.'

At the same forum, Paul Moore, former head of group regulatory risk at Halifax Bank of Scotland, called for 'iconic leaders of personal integrity' in financial services 'whose consciences are finely tuned to requirements of the common good'.

While the accumulation of wealth can lead to the subtlest of temptations—a misplaced sense of security in material possessions—another temptation, particularly amongst the young, is peer pressure—not wanting to be thought of badly by one's friends. It puts the good opinion of others before what is morally right. Many of today's young are particularly good at friendship—at simply being friends to one other. They value loyalty and fidelity in relationships and deplore cheating on one's partner. But, for some, peer pressure can lead to a great deal of unhappiness.

In a feature extract from her book *Living Dolls* (2010), Natasha Walters writes in *The Sunday Times* (10 January 2010) about the sexual liberalization of vulnerable girls and young women (and she might just as well have written the same about young men), released from 'the cage of chastity'. 'But what I heard from some women is that they feel there is now a new cage,' she writes, 'holding them back from the liberation they sought, a cage in which repression of emotions takes the place of repression of physical needs. Many young women seem to feel their lives have been impoverished by the devaluation of sex into exchange and performances... replacing the culture in which sex was associated with the flowering of intimacy. Although it is so often associated with liberation, I am not convinced it is what all feminists were seeking. I kept hearing a frustration from the young women I interviewed, all the sadder because it is so often hidden.'

Walters quotes a 24-year-old woman who told her that 'there was huge pressure on me to join in with that kind of behaviour, but I didn't. That wasn't what I wanted from sex. That kind of casual relationship isn't right for me, but I was made to feel like a freak right through school and university because of it.'

Compare this with the purity of Mary, the mother of Jesus, and the willingness of Joseph, her betrothed husband-to-be, to stick by her when she found she was pregnant.

The sheer persistence of our temptations is why admission or confession is so important for liberation: 'Confess your faults one to another and pray for one another that ye may be healed.' Confession is the shock tactic that overrules or changes the synapses in our brains. It creates shame. We see the full horror of our temptations indulged for what they are. Shame and guilt are no bad things so long as they lead to repentance and an inner sense of forgiveness. Today's society wants to abolish the burden of guilt through excuse rather than through personal change and repentance—the complete turning around of our personalities which sets us free and points us in an entirely different direction. James Jones, the Bishop of Liverpool, writes in his book *Jesus and the Earth* (2003): 'There is good guilt and bad guilt. Bad guilt leads to worthlessness and low self-esteem; good guilt evokes moral responsibility and moral action.'

Buchman used to say that, for him, Charles Wesley's prayer, 'Make and keep me pure with', are the six most important words in the English language. Buchman may have been referring to purity of motive as much as behaviour. He never married and lived a celibate life. He was, as Gandhi would have said, a *Brahmachari*. But he seemed to have an acute awareness of the effect that moral compromise in areas of sexual morality could have on his immediate associates and the wider public. Our sexuality is a gift of God and, as such, should be welcomed as a treasured gift. We needn't be afraid of it. But it needs to be treated as such and come under his control. Many throughout history have sublimated their drives for the sake of the wider good. As Alfred, Lord Tennyson wrote in his poem *Sir Galahad*: 'My strength is as the strength of ten because my heart is pure.' Such purity also gives us clarity of thought and maturity of insight and outlook. It gives us wisdom. And selfless friendship between individuals is vastly different from the self-centred lust of 'I want'.

In an online article headlined 'Purity, freedom and imagination', Dr Philip Boobbyer of the University of Kent warns about the debilitating effect of pornography on people's lives: 'human nature is an integral whole, and what happens in one part of it easily spills over into another. Crossing moral boundaries in one area of life easily leads to the crossing of boundaries in others. Furthermore, a corrupted imagination warps our thinking, and damages our relationships' (www.uk.iofc.org/node/42305).

For myself, I find particular encouragement from the Collect for Purity in Christian liturgy: 'Almighty God, to whom all hearts are open, all desires known, and from whom no secrets are hid; cleans the thoughts of our hearts by the inspiration of Thy holy spirit, that we may perfectly love Thee and worthily magnify Thy holy name through Christ our lord.' If no secrets are hidden from God's gaze—

an alarming prospect—then we can also take comfort from the fact that he goes on loving and forgiving us, regardless.

William Barclay suggests four defences against temptation:

- one's self-respect;
- tradition, part of our heritage that will not allow for compromise;
- the love we hold for our friends and relatives and the love that they hold for us—we would not want to let them down;
- and an awareness of the presence of God, for Christians incarnate in Jesus Christ, in our everyday lives.

I also found helpful instructions on how to deal with temptation in the study guide *The Word for Today* published by United Christian Broadcasters (19 December 2009):

'When it comes to temptation, remember seven things:

1. *Never say 'never'.* You never become so spiritual that you become immune. 'No temptation has overtaken you except such as is common to man; but God is faithful, who will not allow you to be tempted beyond what you are able, but with the temptation will also make the way of escape, that you may be able to bear it' (1 Corinthians 10, v 13 NKJV).

2. *Realise you can stumble on the last lap.* Because you haven't blown it yet, doesn't mean you can't. Satan is a master of timing, and he's in no particular hurry.

3. *Acknowledge your basic drives.* Your flesh is powerful; once indulged it will always want more.

4. *Understand that you are responsible.* Sin is a choice. When you choose to abuse God's grace you pay the price, either now or later. 'Do not be deceived... whatever a man sows, he will also reap' (Galatians 6, v 7 NKJV).

5. *You're not a helpless pawn.* You may not be able to change what happened yesterday, but your choice, empowered by God's grace, will determine what happens today and tomorrow.

6. *If you've sinned, there's hope.* God will forgive you and use you again. Jesus told Peter, '... I have prayed for you, that your faith should not fail; and when you have returned to Me, strengthen your brethren' (Luke 22, v 32 NKJV).

7. *Stay safe by staying close to God.* '... Submit to God. Resist the devil and he will flee from you.' (James 4, v 7 NKJV).'

Finally, note also the collective again in this part of the Lord's Prayer: 'Lead *us* not into temptation but deliver *us* from evil.' For temptation indulged is never just a private, personal matter but invariably has an effect on, and consequences for, others. How many lives around us are blighted by our indulgencies? We should not be a source of temptation for others but a source of inspiration and encouragement to them. The tempter is on the get in relationships. The redeemer only sees the best for the other person and wants the best for them.

QUESTIONS:
What tempts me most?
What is my attitude towards pride? Towards money?
What do I place my faith in?
How do I resist temptation?
What strategies can I employ to do so?

9 ...but deliver us from evil

IF WE ARE serious about the need to confront evil, we need to be aware of it both at a personal level and in the world's power structures.

At the personal level, the notion that succumbing to temptation might lead us to evil should be enough to put the fear of God into us—to set off alarm bells. That it doesn't indicates just how seductively attractive temptation is. We forget that 'all that glitters is not gold'. What might be originally good and honourable can too easily be corrupted by our base instincts and motives. We start by justifying to ourselves that our indulgencies don't matter. Drinking turns into alcoholism, the roulette wheel turns into a gambling habit, over-eating turns into obesity, now so severe in the West that it even threatens world food supplies.

Such evils are self-inflicted. Drug, alcohol and tobacco abuse can kill. Dedicated doctors and nurses have to treat the diseases we sometimes inflict on ourselves, even though our life-style choices can become a drain on the public purse. Likewise, prison populations overflow with those who have simply made the wrong choices in life. Barry Mizen, who launched the Jimmy Mizen Foundation in memory of his 16-year-old son after his murder in 2008, comments that 'many young people in prison are not bad people—they have just made terrible decisions.' Prison chaplains do their best to rehabilitate offenders, knowing that it is an uphill task. The punishment of prison may fit the crime. But it often falls far too short in transforming prisoners' lives and too many reoffend after being released.

Young prisoners need to experience forgiveness and healing, says Sarah Tranter, Community Links manager at HM Prison/Young Offenders Institution Rochester, and for that they also need to forgive themselves.*

Like the compass bearing of an aircraft or an oil tanker, we only have to be out by one degree to be steering in the wrong direction in life. We end up miles away from our true destination. Repentance and forgiveness may close the triangle back to where we should be. But we may also have to retrace our steps back to the starting point to see where we went wrong in the first place.

Of course, not all illnesses are a consequence of our lifestyle choices. Someone I know suffered from clinical depression which went undiagnosed for 18 months. He says:

It followed a bout of 'flu. When I thought I had recovered I went to a swimming pool, returning home afterwards in the cold of winter. As I walked home I felt a dark cloud come over my mind. Others who have suffered from depression call it 'the black dog'. Perhaps I should never have gone for that swim. But from then on I felt constantly tired, suffered from stomach cramps and was prone to weeping for no real reason. At the same time I had the sweetest of dreams at night only to wake up to the 'black dog' descending again. The doctors sent me for barium meal tests in case I had developed cancer. Eventually a friend suggested I should see a Christian psychiatric doctor. With great sensitivity, she recognized what had happened to me. She put me on a course of pills and told me that I would begin to feel better after three weeks. I would need to keep taking the pills for six months. She was accurate in her forecast of my recovery to the day. I began to feel noticeably better. She told me

*Tranter was speaking at a Greencoat Forum, London, on 21 February 2012

that no amount of lifting myself up by my own boot-straps or spiritual diagnosis would have made the slight-est difference. I had been suffering from a chemical imbalance in my system and that needed addressing medically. It was as simple as that. If there was any evil in the situation it was that I had been overworking prior to my illness, and that it took so long before a doctor correctly diagnosed my condition. There were times when I felt I was in the depths of hell. I was lucky that I had a friend who cared for me enough to point me towards help and the cure.

Evil is not a popular notion, at least not in the sense that it can reside in us or suddenly attack us. Psychology encourages us to feel good about ourselves. Asked how we are by friends and relatives, we often reply, 'I'm good'. We mean that we are fine/well/okay/happy. Jesus has a startling response to a rich young ruler who asks him, 'Good teacher, what must I do to inherit eternal life?' Instead of immediately answering the question, Jesus replies: 'Why do you call me good? No one is good except God alone.' (Luke 18, vv 18-19, ESV). The implication is not that Jesus is less than divine. On the contrary, it implies that the rich young man may have recognized something of the divinity in Jesus. Jesus seems to be asking him, is this so? Have you recognized my divinity? Is this why you call me good? Why else would you call me good?

No one is good except God alone. We are all fallible, we all fall short of the ideal, we are all in this together. We need to acknowledge, in humility, that sin and wickedness can all too easily overtake us. Evil thoughts can occupy our minds. Yet those who flirt with evil risk being eaten up by it. We harbour anger and bitterness, justifying ourselves in our self-righteousness; we fantasize about opportunities driven by lust, money, power, revenge, material acquisition. We rehearse conversations in our minds—of revenge or seduction, for instance—that would divert ourselves and others from the narrow and straight path and which in reality are best left unsaid. For what is said can never be unsaid. And transparency sometimes needs to be tempered by discretion, such as in the holding of confidences.

But we also need to know that we are redeemed and forgiven sinners. We don't have to go around in sackcloth and ashes; we can all claim 'the glorious liberty of the children of God', and the release from guilt in the knowledge and acceptance of being forgiven. What this supplication in the Lord's Prayer is all about is a plea to liberate us from our fallen human nature; a plea to be transformed.

Indeed, while we should be aware of the power of evil, paradoxically we don't need to be afraid of it, knowing that God can deliver us from evil. As Psalm 23 puts it: 'Even though I walk through the valley of the shadow of death, I will fear no evil, for you are with me; your rod and your staff they comfort me.' (v 4, NIV).

But we also need to acknowledge that forces of evil can be let loose in the world which, if unchecked in human nature, lead to dreadful loss of life and destruction. Millions die at the hands of ruthless dictators. From Hitler's gas chambers and Stalin's purges to the killing fields of Cambodia and Rwanda, millions have been delivered into evil, either as victims or perpetrators.

A Norwegian anti-immigration terrorist, with a distorted notion of national identity, bombs and shoots dead 77 people, most of them teenagers; two pre-teenagers, brought up on a diet of extreme video nasties, kill a toddler on Merseyside; a landscape architect murders his neighbour after watching websites of violent pornography including strangulation. Evil can grip individuals with such overpowering obsessions that they distort any notion of right and wrong and in extreme cases lead to death.

The only thing one can say in the face of such horrors is that Christ suffered too. He may have urged us to pray to be delivered from evil, but he wasn't himself. He prayed not to have to 'drink the cup', yet 'not my will but Thine be done'. In being obedient unto death through crucifixion, he also gained the victory of resurrection and entered into paradise. We too can only hope those who have suffered ultimate evil at the hands of others will also enter into the paradise of the eternal kingdom.

We may all need to be liberated, at one time or another, from unhealthy habits or the obsessions of our fallen human natures, if we are to live with truly liberated and confident personalities. This is the meaning of deliverance from evil. Once again, we are pointed to the only power that can truly liberate us: that of our Father, God in heaven.

Then there is the evil of the world's unjust economic power structures which further impoverish the poorest.

Raymond Baker, the US anti-corruption campaigner and author of *Capitalism's Achilles' Heel*, exposes the corrupt forces still at work in the 'underbelly' of macro-finance and governance, where gateways are left open by mainstream financial institutions, allowing the flow of 'dirty money'. Governments, he says, need to shut down these offshore tax havens used by corrupt individuals to bleed the wealth of poor countries, causing further poverty, human insecurity and misery.

Another form of corruption, he says, is robbing the poor to pay the rich. Over 60 per cent of global illicit money transfers are through commercial tax evasion and false invoicing known as 'transfer pricing'. Goods that are sold in developing countries are invoiced at a higher price than their worth, with the excess funds transferred to offshore bank accounts in places such as the Cayman Islands. The world's 91 tax havens, he says, constitute 'the biggest loophole in the global economic system'.

The entire structure of moving money from the poor world to the rich world, Baker says, is 'cutting the heart out of foreign aid'. The $50–$80 billion a year in official foreign aid is outweighed 10-fold by money flowing in the other direction. The priority, he says, is to restore economic justice through legislation. 'It's not rocket science but it's largely a question of political will.'*

Much has already been written about the failures of the global banking system, fuelled by excessive competitiveness and risk taking, and obsession with making huge sums of money. The financial crash of 2008 led to a 20 per cent drop in world trade and threw 100 million people into poverty, while 8.5 million people lost their jobs in the USA alone. Again we are reminded of St Paul's warning that 'the love of money is the root of all evil'. Sebastian Faulks, in his novel *One week in December*, implies that such greed is more dangerous to the world than the threat of terrorism.

In his book *God doesn't do waste* (2010), Dave Bookless, the founder in the UK of the A Rocha Christian nature conservation organization, writes, 'I am not prone to finding demons in every corner, but as a minister I've seen enough of the effects of evil to take it very seriously when I do encounter it. Much of the greatest evil in today's world is institutional—tied up in worshipping false gods of money and power.... The most effective weapons in a spiritual battle are spiritual ones, and prayer is the most powerful.'

Reflecting on this petition to 'deliver us from evil' in the

---

*Baker was addressing a conference on 'Trust and Integrity in the Global Economy' in Caux, Switzerland, July 2008. See also the book *Treasure Islands* by Nicholas Shaxson (2012), about the world's network of tax havens, who quotes Baker as saying that 'for every dollar that we have been generously handing out across the top of the table, we in the West have been taking back some $10 of illicit money under the table. There is no way to make this formula work for everyone, poor or rich.'

Lord's Prayer, Pope Benedict XVI warns, above all, against the loss of faith in God (*Jesus of Nazareth*, 2007):

> Today... there is also the ideology of success, of well-being, that tells us, 'God is just a fiction, he only robs us of our time and our enjoyment of life. Don't bother with him! Just try to squeeze as much out of life as you can.' These temptations seem irresistible as well. The Our Father in general and this petition in particular are trying to tell us that is only when you have lost God that you have lost yourself; then you are nothing more than a random product of evolution. Then the 'dragon' really has won. So long as the dragon cannot wrest God from you, your deepest being remains unharmed, even in the midst of all the evils that threaten you.... This is why we pray that, in our concern for goods, we don't lose the Good itself; that even faced with the loss of goods, we may not also lose the Good, which is God; that we ourselves may not be lost: Deliver us from evil!

So how do we protect ourselves from the power of evil that can invade our human nature as well as the world's power structures? How do we transcend human nature's dark side? How do we, as Revd David Marshall-Jones says, 'put our secret sins to death'? How do we 'number our days aright, that we may gain a heart of wisdom'? (Psalm 90, v 12, NIV.)

First by acknowledgement. We cannot pretend that evil doesn't exist. Indeed it helps to personify evil, just as our anthropomorphic God is personified in Jesus. We call fallen angels devils, writes Monsignor Roderick Strange (Credo, *The Times,* 2 October 2010). 'They are diabolical. To be diabolical means to tear apart, to rip up, to destroy. When there are movements or forces in society that do untold damage, like genocide or terrorism or abuse, evils that seem driven by a malice we find hard to explain or comprehend, we sometimes call them diabolical.' He continues that 'there can be evil in our midst so severe that it may not be fanciful to ponder its origins. And when we have discovered the human agents, and the historical, political, economic, social, and psychological causes, we may still wonder whether such evil may not have even deeper roots.' The roots lie in the personified Satan himself.

So we should be realistic about the nature of evil. We should call a spade a spade. Jesus is robust indeed. When he warns his disciples about his impending betrayal and crucifixion, the apostle Peter wants to protect him: 'Never, Lord! This shall never happen to you.' Jesus responds: 'Get behind me, Satan! You are a stumbling-block to me; you do not have in mind the things of God, but the things of men.' (Matthew 16, v 23, NIV.) Jesus didn't just say this as a put-down to Peter. In the costly confronting of evil, the slightest hint of a deviation from the price that needs to be paid is also an evil in itself. Evil, then, is anything that deliberately draws us away from the ultimate purposes of God for our lives.

Secondly by personal honesty. Evil scurries for the dark like cockroaches when illuminated by the light of transparency. 'Therefore confess your sins to each other and pray for each other so that you may be healed,' writes the apostle James (James 5, v 16, NIV). Such honesty keeps us humble; it acknowledges that we are all forgiven sinners; without the power of God to protect us we are all prone to evil. Canon J B Phillips writes: 'People will never take evil seriously nor even see much need to tap the resources of God until they join in the costly redemptive purposes of love.' The love that liberates requires us to overcome evil, firstly in ourselves and then in the other person.

Thirdly, as Dave Bookless says, by prayer. We can hastily turn to prayers, in the face of temptations and of evil, of which the Lord's Prayer is the greatest. It helps to commit prayers to memory that are easy to repeat to oneself in times of trial or at any time during the day or night: 'Jesus Christ, son of God, have mercy upon me, a sinner'; 'Cleanse the thoughts of our hearts by the inspiration of thy Holy Spirit that we may perfectly love thee and worthily magnify thy holy name' (Collect for purity, the Book of Common Prayer); 'O God, come to my assistance, O Lord, make haste to help me'; 'Lead us not into temptation but deliver us from evil'; 'Thy kingdom come on earth as it is in heaven'; 'Give us this day our daily bread.' By drawing on such supplications we can decisively reject evil and all its ways.

Finally, we can work together strategically to challenge what is wrong in society and the wider world, in campaigns and mass movements—such as the successful Jubilee 2000 campaign for international debt remission—in parliament, in the media and in our places of work. It is what William Wilberforce MP and his colleagues did successfully in their 20-year campaign to abolish the evils of the slave trade and eventually slavery itself in England and the USA.

The most fearless of all in speaking truth to power, for he surely knew what the consequences would be, was Jesus himself. Six times he repeatedly berates the authorities for their exercise of power and control: 'Woe to you, teachers of the law and Pharisees, you hypocrites!' as vividly reported verbatim by St Matthew in his gospel, chapter 23. 'Woe to you, blind guides,' Jesus throws in for good measure and concludes: 'You snakes! You brood of vipers! How will you escape being condemned to hell?' (v 33, NEV). No wonder they wanted to get rid of him.

In all of this, the Beatitudes are also a great source of encouragement: 'Blessed are the poor in spirit, for theirs is the kingdom of heaven; Blessed are those who mourn, for they shall be comforted; Blessed are the meek, for they will inherit the earth; Blessed are those who hunger and thirst after righteousness, for they will be satisfied; Blessed are the merciful, for they will be shown mercy; Blessed are the pure in heart for they shall see God; Blessed are the peacemakers, for they will be called sons of God.' (Matthew 5, vv 3-10, NIV).

A colleague in Geneva, Andrew Stallybrass, has written this prayer:

> *Our Father, when I look back, I see so much suffering—a history of human evil written in blood. I look at our world, at the newspaper headlines, and the TV news, and I see so many signs of suffering, of evil at work.*
>
> *But may evil never progress through me.*
>
> *In our families, in our nations, there are so many unhealed wounds, hates that are passed on from generation to generation.*
>
> *But may hate never progress through me.*
>
> *There is such a need for sharing and for love.*
>
> *May love and sharing and grace progress through me.*
>
> *Purify me; use my hands, my intelligence, my imagination, to further your kingdom, the true humanity, bound together by mercy, justice, compassion and life. Amen*

QUESTIONS:
What is my picture of evil?
What evil exists in the world?
What evil power structures need to be tackled?
Is there any hidden evil or Achilles' heel in me?
Do I have any secret sins that I need to admit to myself and confess to God?

In the Roman Catholic tradition, the Lord's Prayer ends here, but we shall conclude these reflections with the final sentence used in the Protestant and non-conformist churches.

10. For thine is the kingdom, the power and the glory, for ever and ever, Amen.

WE HAVE come full circle. We are back to the acknowledgement implicit in 'Thy kingdom come on earth...', that all human power structures are subservient to the kingdom of God. Remember the context: the Jews were living under the *Pax Romana* of Augustus Caesar whose earthly power stretched throughout the whole known Western world of that time. While it was a period of superficial peace, the military might of Rome ruthlessly put down any hint of insurrection. As Tom Wright says: 'Power was now concentrated in the hands of one man, whose kingdom stretched from shore to shore.... A kingdom of absolute power, bringing glory to the man at the top.' No wonder, also, that Herod in Jerusalem was worried by what the wise men told him about the birth of a new king. 'If someone had told Augustus what the angels had said to the shepherds, he'd have been worried too.' (Luke 2, vv 8-20.) Jesus, says Wright, 'represents the dangerous alternative, the possibility of a different empire, a different power, a different glory, a different peace.'

The final declaration of the great prayer challenges the very authority of human power. There is no greater power in the world, the prayer asserts, than the power of God at work in the lives of individuals and in the world as a whole. If this is subversive, it is also revolutionary. Kingdoms and empires may rise and fall; emperors, kings and presidents come and go. But the great constant is the robust power of God and his kingdom; not only in this day and age, but throughout the whole human story, the whole of history and for all eternity.

If the Kingdom belongs to God, then so too does the whole of creation. This revolutionizes our attitudes towards possessions. It goes to the very heart of materialism. We can never ever again say, 'What's mine is my own.' We are simply stewards of God's creation. It affects our attitudes towards goods, money—and our use of time. It also revolutionizes our attitude towards the environment—our care and tendering of it—and how we leave the world for future generations. Dave Bookless again: 'I had been especially challenged by meditating on Psalm 24, v 1, which simply reminds us that "The earth is the Lord's and everything in it." What if that assertion, that it is God's world and not ours, really filtered through to our lifestyle choices? What if our shopping, our travel, our attitudes towards money, income and possessions really reflected God's ownership of creation?'

Everything is changed. In losing our claims to ownership, our separate autonomy, our love of money, wealth, possessions and power, we find our true selves. Paradoxically, in letting go we find the fulfilment we all long for. In declaring this final line of the Lord's Prayer we are acknowledging that all good that we do in life is done because of the presence of God in our lives. The glory is his and his alone.

QUESTIONS:
What are the implications of the kingdom, power and
    glory belonging to God?
What does this imply for the world's power structures?
Does God have power in my life?
How do I gain God's power in my life?

* * * * *

Postscript

So what is missing from the Lord's Prayer? It is, of course, an impertinent question. But we can notice that there is no mention of love. The word doesn't arise. Elsewhere Christ affirms that the greatest of all the commandments is to 'Love the Lord your God with all your heart and with all your soul and with all your strength and with all your mind; and love your neighbour as yourself.' (Luke 10, v 27, NIV). On these two commandments, he says, hang all the previous laws and prophets of the Israelites. They are, of course, commands rather than prayers, which are more in the nature of supplications and conversations with God.

What the Lord's Prayer tells us is *how* to love God and our neighbour, the practice of love and not just the emotion of love. You can't hallow God's name, for instance, without first loving him. Hallowing, or holding in the highest honour, is a form of love. You can't worship without love. A man in the hyperbole of love may say to his lover: 'I worship the very ground you stand on.' The Lord's Prayer says, in effect, love God first and all other loves fall into place. As Pope Benedict XVI (*Jesus of Nazareth*, 2007) writes, the 'thou petitions' and the 'we petitions' of the Lord's Prayer are essentially 'explications of the two parts of the great commandment to love God and our neighbour—in other words, they are directions towards the path of love.'

They are also directions to the path of fulfilment: 'I have come that they may have life, and have it to the full.' (John 10, v 10, NIV.)

* * * * *

What does it mean to you?

In the tiny church of St Enodoc near the beach at Trebetheric in Cornwall I found this instructive message about the Lord's Prayer pinned on the noticeboard:

Our Father who are in Heaven
Don't say 'Father' if you don't behave like a son or a daughter. Don't say 'Our' if you only ever think of yourself.

Hallowed by thy Name
Don't say 'Hallowed' if you don't honour that name.

Thy Kingdom come
Don't say 'Thy Kingdom come' if you are weighed down only with material considerations.

Thy will be done
Don't say 'Thy will be done' if you don't accept the hard bits.

On Earth as it is in Heaven
Don't say 'As it is in Heaven' if you only ever think about earthly matters.

Give us this day our daily bread
Don't say 'our daily bread' if you have no concern for the hungry or the homeless.

Forgive us our trespasses as we forgive those who trespass against us.
Don't say 'Forgive us our trespasses' if you remain angry with your fellows.

Lead us not into temptation
Don't say 'Lead us not into temptation' if you intend to continue sinning.

But deliver us from evil

Don't say 'Deliver us from evil' if you won't make a stand against injustice.

For thine is the kingdom, the Power and the Glory, for ever and ever, Amen.

Don't say 'Amen' without considering the words of your prayer.

It may be one of the few prayers that we know by heart, but we need to let its words live in our hearts and our minds.

Bibliography

William Barclay: *The Lord's Prayer: what the Bible tells us about the Lord's Prayer*, St Andrew Press, 2008

Dave Bookless: *God doesn't do waste: redeeming the whole of life*, Inter-Varsity Press, 2010

Gordon Brown: *Beyond the Crash: overcoming the first crisis of globalization*, Simon & Schuster, 2010

Sister Ruth Burrows OCD: *Essence of Prayer*, Burns & Oats, 2006

Stephen Cherry: *Barefoot Disciple: walking the way of passionate humility*, Continuum, 2010

Ken Costa: *God at Work: living every day with purpose*, Continuum, 2007

C H Dodd: *The Founder of Christianity*, Macmillan, USA, 1970, Fontana, UK, 1973.

Tania Ellis: *The New Pioneers: sustainable business success through social innovation and social entrepreneurship*, John Wiley and Sons, *2010*

David Erdal: *Beyond the corporation: humanity working*, The Bodley Head, 2011

Michael Henderson: *No enemy to conquer: forgiveness in an unforgiving* world, Baylor University Press, 2009. See also his website: www.*mh.iofc.org*

Roger Hicks: *The Lord's Prayer and Modern Man*, Blandford Press, 1967

Leif Hovelsen: *Out of the Evil Night,* Blandford Press, 1959

James Jones: *Jesus and the Earth*, SPCK, 2003

Michael Marshall: *The transforming power of prayer: from illusion to reality,* Continuum, 2011

John Munro, *Calm before coffee*, Munro, 2012

Joseph Ratzinger, Pope Benedict XVI: *Jesus of Nazareth*, Bloomsbury, UK, 2007

E F Scott: *The Lord's Prayer*, Charles Scribner's Sons, New York, 1951

Nicholas Shaxson: *Treasure Islands: tax havens and the men who stole the world*, Vintage Books, 2012

Ray Simpson: *The Cowshed Revolution*, subtitled, *A new society created by downardly mobile Christians*, Keven Mayhew Ltd, UK, 2011

Tom Wright: *Simply Christian*, SPCK, 2006

Tom Wright: *The Lord and His Prayer*, Triangle (SPCK), 1996

Philip Yancy: *What's so amazing about grace?* Zondevan, 2000

About the author

Michael Smith has been associated for over 45 years with Initiatives of Change, the international non-governmental organization which aims to build relationships of trust across the world's divides (www.iofc.org). He has served on its UK management board since 2010, where he is Head of Business Programmes. He is the author of *Trust and Integrity in the Global Economy*, a collection of stories of best practice in business and social entrepreneurship, and of *The Sound of Silence*, a booklet aimed at encouraging today's web-surfing generation to take time out each day for silent reflection (www.soundofsilence.org). In the 1970s he worked for three years in India as production manager for the newsweekly magazine *Himmat* in Mumbai and has since made 11 visits to India. He was a founding co-editor of *For A Change* magazine, published by Initiatives of Change, where he worked for 17 years from 1987 to 2004. He has written over 40 obituaries of the pioneers of Initiatives of Change for national newspapers and is an honorary member of the Texas-based International Association of Obituarists. He and his wife, Jan, live in Wimbledon, where he is an Elder at Trinity United Reformed Church. They have two grown-up children.